THE DIALECTS OF ENGLAND

Second Edition

Peter Trudgill

BLACKWELL
Publishers

First published 1990
First published in paperback 1992
Reprinted 1993, 1994, 1998

This second edition published 1999

Blackwell Publishers Ltd
108 Cowley Road
Oxford OX4 1JF
UK

Blackwell Publishers Inc
350 Main Street
Malden, Massachusetts 02148
USA

British Library Cataloguing in Publication Data
A CIP catalogue record for this book is available from the British Library.

Library of Congress Cataloging in Publication Data
Trudgill, Peter
    The dialects of England / Peter Trudgill. — 2nd ed.
        p.   cm.
    Includes bibliographical references and index.
    ISBN 0–631–21814–9 (hardback : acid-free paper). — ISBN
0–631–21815–7 (pbk. : acid-free paper)
        1. English language—Dialects—England.   2. English language—
Social aspects—England.   I. Title.
PE1711.T74   1999
427—dc21   99–36555
                                                                      CIP

Typeset in 11 on 12.5pt Ehrhardt
by Ace Filmsetting Ltd
Printed in Great Britain by MPG Books Ltd, Bodmin, Cornwall

This book is printed on acid-free paper.

Contents

———◆———

Maps

———◆———

Preface to the Second Edition

◆

This revised edition of *The Dialects of England* contains the usual updatings, revisions and clarifications, but it also differs from the first edition by the inclusion of phonetic symbols. The original orthographic representations of speech sounds have been retained for the benefit of those without any training in phonetics, but, at the request of many readers who are familiar with and perhaps more comfortable with the alphabet of the International Phonetics Association, these symbols have been added to the text at appropriate points.

The author would like to thank the many people who corresponded with him about the first edition of this book and sent him information about their local dialects, especially Mr Vic Woods of Redcar.

Fribourg, April 1999

Acknowledgements

◆

The author and publishers wish to thank the following for permission to use copyright material: Antique Collectors' Club Ltd, for 'The Tawny Owl' from *Tha's a Rum'un, Bor* by John Kett, Baron Publishing, 1973, and 'An Ordinerry Rood' from *Tha's a Rum'un Tew* by John Kett, Baron Publishing, 1975. John Benjamins B. V., for maps from David North, 'Spatial aspects of linguistic change in Surrey, Kent and Sussex' in W. Viereck, ed., *Focus on England and Wales*, pp. 94 and 92, 1985. The C. W. Daniel Company Ltd, for an extract from 'Riches' by Bernard Moore, 1933. Richard Kay Publications, for an extract from G. E. Campion, 'Noa Callers' from *Lincolnshire Dialects*, 1976. Northern Songs, for extracts from 'I Saw Her Standing There' by John Lennon and Paul McCartney, *c*.1963, and 'I've Just Seen a Face' by John Lennon and Paul McCartney, *c*.1960. Devina Symes, for 'The Christmas Partee' from *Here in Dorset: Poetry by Devina Symes*, 1980.

1

Language Variety in England

One thing that is important to very many English people is *where they are from*. For many of us, whatever happens to us in later life, and however much we move house or travel, the place where we grew up and spent our childhood and adolescence retains a special significance. Of course, this is not true of all of us. More often than in previous generations, families may move around the country, and there are increasing numbers of people who have had a nomadic childhood and are not really 'from' anywhere. But for a majority of English people, pride and interest in the area where they grew up is still a reality. The country is full of football supporters whose main concern is for the club of their childhood, even though they may now live hundreds of miles away. Local newspapers criss-cross the country in their thousands on their way to 'exiles' who have left their local areas. And at Christmas time the roads and railways are full of people returning to their native heath for the holiday period.

Where we are from is thus an important part of our personal identity, and for many of us an important component of this local identity is the way we speak – our accent and dialect. Nearly all of us have regional features in the way we speak English, and are happy that this should be so, although of course there are upper-class people who have regionless accents, as well as people who for some reason wish to conceal their regional origins. The vast majority of the population, however, speak in a manner which identifies them as coming from a particular place. They speak like the people they grew up with, and in a way that is different from people who grew up somewhere else. Of course, people may change the way in which they speak during their lifetimes, especially if they move around the country, but most of us carry at least some trace of our accent and dialect origins with us all of our lives. Other people will use this information to help them decide where we are from, and will say things like 'You must be a Londoner', 'You sound as if you're a southerner', 'Whereabouts in Scotland are you from?', 'I can't quite place your accent', or 'You're from Yorkshire, aren't you?'. And labels for people of different regional origins are freely used – you can get called 'Geordie', 'Cockney', 'Jock', 'Taffy', 'Scouse', and so on, depending on what you sound like when you speak.

This book on English dialects is about this variety in the way we speak English, and it is about the way *all* of us who are from England speak our native language, because *all* of us speak with an accent, and *all* of us speak a dialect. Your accent is the way in which you pronounce English, and since all of us pronounce when we speak, we all have an accent. Some accents, it is true, are more regional than others. Some people have very regional accents, so that you can tell exactly where they come from if you are clever enough at spotting accents. Other people have fewer regional features, and you might be able to place them only approximately – 'You're from somewhere in the West Country, but I can't tell where.' And yet other people may have very few regional features at all, so that you might be reduced to saying something as vague as 'You're a southerner.' There are even a small number of people – probably between 3 and 5 per cent of the population of England – who have a totally regionless accent. These are usually people who have been to one of the big Public Schools, or who want to sound as if they have. This accent is sometimes referred to as a 'BBC accent' because readers of the national news on radio and television are usually selected from this minority of the population.

Similarly, everybody also speaks a dialect. When we talk about **dialect** we are referring to something more than accent. We are referring not only to pronunciation but also to the words and grammar that people use. Thus if you say

I haven't got any

and I say

I ain't got none

you and I differ in the grammar we use, and are therefore speaking different dialects. Normally, of course, dialect and accent go together.

2

If you speak Lancashire dialect, you will obviously speak it with a Lancashire accent. But it is worth making a distinction between accent and dialect because of what happens with the important dialect we call Standard English. Standard English is the dialect which is normally used in writing, and which is spoken by the most educated and powerful members of the population: probably no more than 12–15 per cent of the population of England are native speakers of Standard English.

The fact is that everybody who speaks with a BBC accent also speaks the Standard English dialect, like, say, Anna Ford or Alastair Burnett. But not everybody who speaks Standard English does so with a BBC accent. Most people who speak Standard English – perhaps 7–12 per cent of the population of the country – do so with some kind of regional accent, like Melvyn Bragg or John Kettley. This accent and this dialect do not therefore inevitably go together, and it is useful to be able to distinguish, by using the terms dialect and accent, between speakers who do combine them and those who do not.

Standard English is not often referred to as a dialect, but since it is a variety of the language that differs from others in its grammar, it is clearly just as much a dialect as any other variety. Standard English uses grammatical forms such as

> I *did* it
> A man *that* I know
> He *doesn't* want *any*
> She *isn't* coming
> We *saw* him

The other, Nonstandard Dialects may use grammatical forms such as

> I *done* it
> A man *what* I know
> He *don't* want *none*
> She *ain't* coming
> We *seen* him

Standard English also comes in a number of different forms around the world. The grammar of American Standard English is obviously a little different from English Standard English. English Standard English speakers say

I haven't written to him even though *I should have done*

Americans would say

I haven't written to him even though *I should have*

English speakers would say

It's *got* cold in here

American Standard English speakers would say

It's *gotten* cold in here

Scottish Standard English is a little different again, of course, and so is Irish Standard English. Within England, however, Standard English is written and spoken more or less the same over the whole country. Standard English speakers from the south of England are more likely to say things like

I won't do it   *We haven't* seen him

than speakers from the north of England, who are more likely to say

I'll not do it   *We've not* seen him

But what regional differences there are are very few.

It is important, too, not to confuse the issue of Standard English versus Nonstandard Dialects with the issue of formal versus informal language. All dialects can be spoken in less or more formal styles, depending on the nature of the situation. If someone says

I'm bloody sozzled

they are speaking an informal style of Standard English. If, on the other hand, they say

I be very drunk

they are speaking a more formal style but of some nonstandard dialect.

4

Like all other dialects, Standard English admits stylistic variation, including the use of swearing and highly informal vocabulary, or **slang**, such as *sozzled*.

In this book we shall not be saying very much about Standard English. Nearly all of the thousands of textbooks, grammars and dictionaries that have been compiled for the English language are already about Standard English, even though most people do not speak this dialect. This book will do only a little to redress this balance, but it is mainly about the *other* dialects of the language. Nor shall we have a lot to say in this book about slang. Rather, we shall be concentrating most closely on the nonstandard, regional dialects to be found in different parts of England, which, as we have seen, are spoken by the vast majority of the population, and which have to do, amongst other things, with where people are from.

Most often, in talking about these regional dialects, we will be concentrating on those social dialects which are most unlike Standard English. In any given area we find a social scale of dialects, with people at the top of the social hierarchy tending to speak Standard English, and with more and more nonstandard regional features occurring as we go down the social hierarchy. We shall be focusing our attention towards the most regional of the varieties.

We shall also be looking at two rather different sorts of dialects. **Traditional Dialects** are what most people think of when they hear the term **dialect**. They are spoken by a probably shrinking minority of the English-speaking population of the world, almost all of them in England, Scotland and Northern Ireland. They are most easily found, as far as England is concerned, in the more remote and peripheral rural areas of the country, although some urban areas of northern and western England still have many Traditional Dialect speakers. These dialects differ very considerably from Standard English, and from each other, and may be difficult for others to understand when they first encounter them. People who say

She bain't a-comin or *Hoo inno comin* or *Her idden comin*
'She's not coming'

are speaking Traditional Dialect. So are people who, for example, pronounce *bone* as 'bee-an' [bɪen] or 'bane' [beːn] or 'bwoon' [bwʊn]. Mainstream Dialects, on the other hand, include both the Standard English Dialect and the Modern Nonstandard Dialects. Most native

English speakers speak some variety of Mainstream Dialect. These dialects are associated with native speakers outside the British Isles, especially in recently settled areas which speak mixed colonial dialects, such as Australia and most of America and Canada. In Britain, they are particularly associated with those areas of the country from which Standard English originally came – the southeast of England; with most urban areas; with places which have become English-speaking only relatively recently, such as the Scottish Highlands, much of Wales, and western Cornwall; with the speech of most younger people; and with middle- and upper-class speakers everywhere. The Mainstream Modern Nonstandard Dialects differ much less from Standard English and from each other, and are often distinguished much more by their pronunciation – their accent – than by their grammar. Mainstream Dialect speakers might say, for example,

She's not coming or *She isn't coming* or *She ain't comin*

They might also pronounce the word *bone* as 'bown' [bæʊn], 'boun' [boʊn] or 'bawn' [bɔːn]. In this book we shall be discussing both the Mainstream Modern Dialects spoken by the majority of the population, and the older, minority Traditional Dialects.

The systematic scientific study of Traditional Dialects began rather late in this country compared to many other European countries, but much of what we shall be saying in this book about Traditional Dialects will be based in part on the very important work of the *Survey of English Dialects.* Inspired and conceived by Harold Orton, and based at the University of Leeds, the *Survey* has been recording and reporting on Traditional Dialects in England since the 1950s.

Dialect Areas

People often ask: how many dialects are there in England? This question is impossible to answer. After all, how many places are there to be from? If you travel from one part of the country to another, you will most often find that the dialects change gradually as you go. The further you travel, the more different the dialects will become from the one in the place where you started, but the different dialects will seem to merge into one another, without any abrupt transitions.

There are no really sharp dialect boundaries in England, and dialects certainly do not coincide with counties. Yorkshire Dialect, for instance, does not suddenly change dramatically into Durham Dialect as you cross the County Durham boundary. Indeed, the dialects of northern Yorkshire are much more like those of County Durham than they are like those of southern Yorkshire. Dialects form a continuum, and are very much a matter of more-or-less rather than either/or. There is really no such thing as an entirely separate, self-contained dialect. Dialectologists often draw lines on maps dividing areas which have a particular word or pronunciation from those which don't. If they then put all these lines together on a single map, they find that none of them are in exactly the same place. Dialects differ from immediately neighbouring dialects only slightly, and can be heard to change slowly and word by word, pronunciation by pronunciation, as you travel from one village to the next.

All the same, in this book we shall be talking about Traditional Dialect and Modern Dialect areas *as if* there were such things as separate dialects. This is a convenient thing to do. We realize that dialects form a continuum, but for the sake of clarity and brevity, we divide this continuum up into areas at points where it is least continuum-like. That is, we draw boundaries between dialect areas at places where we find a situation most closely resembling an abrupt transition. This has the advantage of fitting in with most people's perceptions of how dialects work. After all, if you can tell a Liverpudlian from a Mancunian by their speech, it will not necessarily worry you that there may be places between Liverpool and Manchester whose dialects you will have trouble in placing. However, in our discussions of dialect areas, it must always be borne in mind that these areas are not particularly firmly or permanently fixed, and that they can only be a simplified approximation to what actually happens in real life. The lines we draw on our maps dividing one dialect area from another cannot easily be located at any precise point on the M4 motorway, the London-to-Carlisle railway line, or anywhere else.

Origins of Dialect Differences

One very interesting question that is often asked is: where do different dialects come from? Why are there dialects? Why is it that people in different parts of the country speak differently? This is a difficult as well as interesting question to answer, and one that we shall be tackling in later chapters also. The question is probably easier to answer if we turn it round and ask: why doesn't everybody in every part of England speak the same? The answer is that English, like all other languages in the world, is constantly changing, and that different changes take place in different parts of the country. A change may start in a particular location and spread out from there to cover neighbouring areas. Some of these changes may spread so much that they eventually cover the whole country. More often, though, changes will only spread so far, leading to dialect differences between areas which have the new form and areas which do not.

Often the spread of changes will be halted by barriers to communication such as countryside which is difficult to cross. One of the most important dialect boundaries in England runs through the Fens, which until quite recently was an isolated, swampy area which was very difficult to get across. It is not an accident therefore that people in Norfolk say *laugh* 'lahf' /laːf/ and *butter* 'butter' /bʌtə/ while people in Lincolnshire say 'laff' /læf/ and 'bootter' /bʊtə/. As we shall see later, the Norfolk pronunciations are newer forms which are the result of changes which never made it across the Fens into Lincolnshire because very few *people* made it across, because of the difficulties of the terrain.

Language change is one of the most mystifying and fascinating phenomena that dialectologists and linguistic scientists encounter. Sometimes we can explain language change by reference to external factors: it is easy to account for the wholesale adoption by the English language of very large numbers of originally French words by referring to the Norman Conquest of England by French-speaking rulers in 1066. But more often than not there is no such explanation, and we have to say simply that it appears to be a natural characteristic of human languages that they change – in pronunciation and grammar as well as vocabulary. We are especially bad at explaining why a particular language change occurs when and where it does rather than in some other place and at some other time.

If we look far enough back in time we can see that it is often change in language that has led to the growth of different languages in the first place. The fact is that the languages we today call Swedish, Danish, Norwegian, Icelandic, Faroese, German, Dutch, Frisian and English were, around 2,000 years or so ago, all the same language. These languages, which form what we now call the Germanic language family, are all descended from a common ancestor of which we have no records. This original Germanic language, in its turn, is derived from an ancestor language which is often called Indo-European, which was spoken somewhere in Eurasia perhaps 6,000 years ago, and which is the parent language not only of Germanic but also of Hindi, Bengali, Persian, Sinhalese and nearly all the languages of Europe including Russian, Lithuanian, Greek, Albanian, Italian and Welsh.

The break-up of the original Indo-European language into its modern descendants, and of the original Germanic language into English, German, etc., were caused by the same phenomenon – language change. What happened was that the language changed but that it changed in different ways in different places. The more time that elapsed, the more the language changed, and the more the different varieties of the language drifted apart, until the descendants of people who long ago all spoke the same language today speak many different languages, most of which are totally mutually incomprehensible. We can see that, for example, Dutch and Norwegian come from the same family of languages as English when we notice the many similarities that exist between them, such as:

Dutch	Norwegian	English
twee	to	two
drie	tre	three
huis	hus	house
man	mann	man
brood	brød	bread

But English speakers can still not understand Dutch or Norwegian without first studying them. A thousand years ago they probably would have been able to.

This same mechanism has been at work within the English language itself ever since it was first brought to Britain by Germanic-speaking invaders and settlers about 1,500 years ago. Even then the language was not at all uniform. But over the intervening centuries the English language has changed enormously, with the result that the Old English or Anglo-Saxon language as written by King Alfred is no longer comprehensible to us, and the mediaeval Middle English of Chaucer is by no means easy to read, and would be even harder to understand if we could hear it spoken.

As the language has changed in this way, it has changed in different ways in different parts of the country, with the result that, as the centuries have gone by, differences between the dialects have increased. The fact that English has been spoken in England for 1,500 years but in Australia for only 200 explains why we have a great wealth of regional dialects in England that is more or less totally lacking in Australia. It is often possible to tell where an English person comes from to within about 15 miles or less. In Australia, where there has not been enough time for changes to bring about much regional variation, it is almost impossible to tell where someone comes from at all, although very small differences are now beginning to appear.

The Future

It is unlikely, however, that there will ever be as much dialectal variation in Australia as there is in England. This is because modern transport and communications conditions are very different from what they were 1,500 or even 100 years ago. Even though English is now spoken in many different parts of the world many thousands of miles apart, it is very unlikely that English will ever break up into a number of different non-intelligible languages in the same way that Indo-European and Germanic did. German and Norwegian became different languages because the ancestors of the speakers of these two languages moved apart geographically, and were no longer in touch and communicating with one another. In the modern world, barring unforeseen catastrophes, this will not happen, at least in the near future. As long as Americans and British people, for instance, are in touch with one another and want to communicate with one another, it is most unlikely that their dialects will drift so far apart as to become different languages.

It is equally unlikely, however, that we will ever all end up speaking the same dialect. From time to time, people who ought to know better predict that in fifty years' time all British and Australian people will be speaking American English just like the Americans. This is clearly nonsense. What is actually happening to the different varieties of English seems to be this. At the moment, American and English English are diverging in their pronunciation. In many respects, American and English accents are slowly getting more unlike one another. This is because changes in pronunciation are taking place in America which are not happening in England, and vice versa. To take just one example, there is a growing tendency in American English to pronounce words like *man* as 'mee-an' [mɪən] which is not found at all in Britain. Similarly, there is a growing tendency in Britain to pronounce words like *better* as 'be'er' [bɛʔə], with a glottal stop (see p. 77), which is not found in America.

It may well be, therefore, that in 100 years' time the different accents will take a little more getting used to, and a little more concentration, if we are to understand one another. It must be borne in mind, though, that familiarity always breeds greater understanding. When talking-films were first introduced into Britain from the United States, very many people complained that they could not understand them. This may seem very strange to us now, but of course until the 1930s the vast majority of British people had never heard an American accent. Now British people have no trouble in understanding the sort of American English that appears on television because it is so familiar to them.

The same tendency to divergence is probably also occurring in the case of grammar, although it is a little harder to tell what is happening here. The two varieties are in any case very similar grammatically, but it seems that one or two further differences are beginning to emerge, so that it may be that American and British English are moving slightly further apart grammatically, albeit extremely slowly.

On the other hand, American and British English are probably getting more alike when it comes to vocabulary. More and more words are crossing the Atlantic in both directions. Until the 1950s, most British people said *wireless*. Now most say *radio*. Many scores of words now used quite naturally by all British speakers were formerly considered 'Americanisms'. Twenty years ago Americans never used the British and Australasian swear-word *bloody*. Now increasing numbers of them are doing so. And so on.

This difference between what is happening with accents and what is happening with words is quite easy to explain. It is a simple matter to learn new words and expressions and add them to our vocabularies, and all of us do this all our lives. We can even pick up words and phrases from the radio and television, and with so many television programmes crossing from Britain to America and vice versa it is not surprising that words and fashionable phrases cross with them. Pronunciation, on the other hand, is very different. Pronouncing our native dialect is something we all learn how to do very early in life, and it is a very complex business indeed, involving the acquisition of deeply automatic processes which require movements of millimetre accuracy and microsecond synchronization of our lips, jaw, tongue, soft palate and vocal cords. Once this has been learned, it is very difficult indeed to unlearn, which is why nearly all of us have a foreign accent when we try to speak a new language. Accents do not therefore change nearly so readily.

What seems to be necessary for someone to change their accent, even if only slightly, is for them to be in frequent face-to-face contact with speakers with different accents. Scots probably hear London accents on television every day of the week, but they do not acquire any features of a London accent unless they move to London and spend large amounts of time talking to Londoners. Nearly all British people, similarly, are exposed to lots of American English, but the only British people who acquire any features of an American accent are those who spend time in America or otherwise spend a great deal of time interacting with Americans.

The same is true of the role of the electronic media in influencing the spread of linguistic changes within England itself. Television obviously plays a role in influencing the words and phrases people use, but it does not play any important part in influencing their accents or the grammatical structure of their dialects. The point about the television set is that you do not talk to it – and even if you do, it can't hear you.

The answer to the question of whether British and American English are converging or diverging is therefore a complicated one: in some ways they are converging, in other ways they are diverging. Either way, it is nothing to worry about.

The Correctness of Dialects

We have to acknowledge, however, that there are plenty of people who *do* worry about language change. England seems to be full of people who write to the newspapers and the BBC complaining about the way in which the language is 'degenerating', without appearing to realize that the way they speak and write themselves is the result of thousands of years of language change. They complain about 'Americanisms' (which are by definition bad for these complainers), and about 'decay' and 'corruption' in the English language, as well as about 'sloppy speech' and 'bad grammar'. These complaints are a very interesting phenomenon, and one that seems to be repeated in every generation for every language. Although language change is, as we have seen, natural and therefore inevitable, there always seems to be a minority of people who speak the language in question who do not like it. There is of course nothing that they can really do about language change, but they continue to complain all the same.

Sometimes we can explain their horror in social terms. Objections to 'Americanisms' are presumably really objections to what the objectors perceive to be symbolic of a threat to their culture and way of life. (After all, very few people object to the introduction of, say, French words into English, because French culture is not perceived as being threatening.) Similarly, if they object to the increasing use of glottal stops in words like *better* in English, this is presumably because the glottal stop was formerly a feature of lower-social-class dialects which is now beginning to find its way up the social scale in a way that some older middle- and upper-class people might find threatening. In other cases, however, we are simply reduced to saying that there will always be some people who will object to anything that is new just because it is new.

These intolerant people may also in some cases be the same people who are critical of all English dialects other than Standard English. There are a number of people who believe that Standard English is 'correct English', and that all other dialects are 'wrong'. They seem to believe, in fact, that Standard English is *the* English language, and that all other dialects are in some way deviations from or corruptions of Standard English. Historically, of course, this is not true. Standard English has its origins in the older Traditional Dialects of the southeast of England, and rose to prominence because this was the area in which London, Oxford and Cambridge were situated, and which contained the royal court and the government. If the capital of England had been, say, York, then Standard English today would have shown a close resemblance to northern dialects of English.

The fact is that all dialects, both Traditional and Modern, are equally grammatical and correct. They differ only in their social significance and function. As a result of a historical accident, the Standard English dialect is today the dialect which is used in writing, and which, by convention, is used for official purposes. This is why we teach children in British schools to read and write in this dialect. This does not mean, however, that there is anything wrong or linguistically inferior about the other dialects, which, as we have noted, are spoken by, and will undoubtedly continue to be spoken by, the majority of the population of England.

All dialects of English have their own perfectly valid grammars, and we shall be looking at some aspects of these grammatical structures in more detail in chapter 4. The fact that these grammars may differ in some respects from Standard English does not make those grammars wrong or inferior, merely different. In some cases, differences between Standard English and other dialects are due to changes that have taken place in Standard English. An example of this is the retention in the nonstandard dialects of the older negative form, as in

> *I don't want no dinner*

which has been lost in Standard English. In other cases, it may be that Standard English retains older forms which have been lost in other dialects, such as verb forms like

> *I drew a picture*

where certain other dialects might have newer forms such as

> *I drawed a picture*

There is nothing linguistically superior about Standard English. It is not more 'pure' or more correct than other forms of speech. It is not even legitimate to claim that it is more 'acceptable' than other dialects, unless we specify *who* it is acceptable to. There are very many people who find Standard English highly unacceptable, at least in certain situations. The superiority that Standard English has is social. As we said above, we shall not be discussing the Standard English dialect to any great extent in the rest of this book, since it has already been very well and thoroughly described and discussed in our grammar books and our dictionaries.

Differences in Language Use between Dialects

As we have seen, dialects differ in their pronunciation – their accents – and in their grammar and vocabulary. All aspects of the language are important in differentiating between dialects, although, as we have seen, in the case of the Modern Dialects pronunciation is usually the biggest clue as to where someone comes from. There is also one other difference between dialects, however, and one which is not so often discussed as the others. The fact is that dialects also differ in terms of how they are *used* by their speakers. There are different norms in different dialect areas as to how language is supposed to be used, and even what it is for.

Some urban dialect areas, for instance, are known for the ability of their speakers to conduct conversations containing quickfire wit and repartee. This is true, for instance, of Merseyside and of Cockney speakers. In other areas, such as East Anglia, slower speech styles and more sardonic wit is appreciated. This is part of a much wider pattern in the world's languages whereby different communities have different ideas about what is good and bad in the use of language. Differences can be found of many different types: how much people say, how quickly they speak, how loudly they talk, the degree to which they talk to strangers, when and whether they say please and thank-you, and so on.

Within England these differences are usually not big enough to cause serious problems of communication, but they do lead to stereotyping of speakers from certain areas as having certain characteristics. The skilled practitioners of Cockney-style conversations might be valued in London as amusing and interesting, but are readily perceived by speakers in neighbouring East Anglia as being arrogant and dominating. East Anglians are correspondingly perceived by Londoners as being taciturn and unfriendly, but will tell you if asked that they do not like to intrude conversationally where they are not wanted. And so on. Dialects differ in their conversational styles as well as in their accents, grammar and vocabulary. This often emerges in anecdotes and tales about different parts of the country. The following conversation could surely not have taken place in London or Liverpool:

> I was lost in a Norfolk lane, so I stopped a man and I said to him: 'Good morning!'
>
> He looked at me. 'Good morning,' I cried. 'Can you tell me if I am right for Norwich?'
>
> He continued to look at me. Then, in an uneasy, suspicious way, he said: 'What d'ye want to know for?'
>
> I might have been annoyed, but leaning out of the car and putting on an affable expression which I usually keep for tea-parties, I said: 'My dear old bor, I want to know because I want to get to Norwich.'

The ghost of a smile flitted over his rustic face, and he replied after some deep thought, rather reluctantly, and looking away from me: 'Well, you're right!'[1]

Other Dialects and Languages

The dialects of English that we have mentioned so far are the Traditional Dialects of England; and the Mainstream Dialects, including Standard English and the Modern Nonstandard Dialects. These of course account for the majority of the population of the country. But they do not account for the entire population. Many other forms of English, and other languages, are also spoken in modern England.

There are many speakers of overseas varieties of English such as American and Australian present in the country for shorter or longer periods, and speakers of Welsh, Irish and Scottish forms of English are naturally especially numerous. Other forms of English are brought with them by foreign tourists, business people and other visitors such as Germans and Japanese who speak English with different degrees of proficiency, having learnt it for the most part at school as a foreign language, each individual usually aiming as best he or she can at the sort of English that English people speak without actually getting all the way there.

Different from these forms of English are those that have been brought to England by speakers from countries where English is not a foreign but a second language. In countries such as India, Pakistan, Bangladesh, Sri Lanka, Ghana, Nigeria, Sierra Leone, Kenya, Tanzania, Singapore, Malta and many others, English is so widely used as the language of education, government and wider communication, even though there are no or very few native speakers, that distinctive, institutionalized forms of English have developed. Indian English, for instance, as spoken by highly educated Indians, has its own distinctive characteristic words and pronunciations in the same way that American English does.

Different again are the forms of English, now widely spoken in England, that are of Caribbean origin. Some forms are clearly English of a type which is Caribbean in the same way that Canadian English is Canadian and Australian English Australian. Other forms of Caribbean English, sometimes known as 'patois' or 'creole', are so unlike other forms of English that it would be better in some ways to regard them

16

as languages related to English rather than actually English. These fascinating varieties of language derive most of their vocabulary from English. Many of their grammatical structures, however, stem from African languages and from the creativity of speakers from all over West Africa who, during the early years of the Atlantic slave trade, had as their only common language a limited amount of English which they fashioned, out of their own mental resources, into normal languages of considerable subtlety and complexity which nevertheless have an ab-normal history. In some parts of England new forms of creole-influ-enced English are spoken by some people of West Indian origin, and, amongst certain groups of young people, by their non-West Indian friends.

The poem 'Inglan is a Bitch' by the well-known Linton Kwesi Johnson, part of which is given here, is written in a form of English with a number of patois features.

> well mi dbu day wok an mi dhu night wok
> mi dhu clean wok an' mi dhu dutty wok
> dem seh dat black man is very lazy
> but if y'u si how mi wok y'u woulda sey mi crazy
>
> Inglan is a bitch
> dere's no escapin' it
> Inglan is a bitch
> y'u better face up to it
>
> mi know dem have work, work in abundant
> yet still, dem make mi redundant
> now, at fifty-five mi gettin' quite ol'
> yet still, dem sen' me fi goh draw dole
>
> Inglan is a bitch
> dere's no escapin' it
> Inglan is a bitch fi true
> is whey wi a goh dhu 'bout it?[2]

In addition to these forms of English, we have to recognize that many English cities are now very multilingual places, with London's schoolchildren in particular speaking, in addition to English, many scores of different languages as their mother tongue. Languages such as

Panjabi, Gujerati, Bengali, Italian, Greek, Maltese, Chinese, Turkish and many others are very widely spoken in different parts of the country.

These languages have come, of course, from overseas in relatively recent times, but England has a long history of being multilingual. It is a mistake to think of the country as having been entirely English-speaking until modern times. In the early years of this century, for instance, very many speakers of the Jewish language Yiddish were concentrated in the East End of London, and Yiddish still has a number of speakers in the country. Cornish was spoken in western Cornwall until at least the eighteenth century. And in earlier centuries, refugees speaking Dutch and French fled from religious persecution to England and were present here in many cities in very large numbers until they were gradually assimilated linguistically. Norwich, to take just one example, was more than one-third Dutch-speaking in the sixteenth century, and Dutch continued to be spoken there for over 200 years.

Earlier arrivals included the Gypsies, in late mediaeval times, who spoke an Indo-European language originally from northern India, closely related to Panjabi and Hindi, called Romany. Romany is probably not spoken in England any more, but it survives in Wales and is widely spoken by Gypsies all over Europe and in North America. What does, however, survive in England is a very interesting language called Anglo-Romany which consists of Romany words spoken with English grammar and English pronunciation. Here is an extract from St Luke's gospel (15.3–6) in Anglo-Romany:

> Jesus pukkered them this parable: 'Suppose tutti's got a hundred bokros and yek of them's nasherdi. Is there a mush among the lot of you as would not muk the wavver ninety-nine in the bokro-puv and jel after the nasherdi bokro till he latchers it? Karna he's latchered it he riggers it on his dummer, well-pleased he is. Karna he jels home he pukkers his friends and all the foki around: 'Be happy with mandi, because I've found my nasherdi bokero.'[3]

In mediaeval times, too, England was a very multilingual place. In the twelfth century Norwich contained sizeable groups of speakers of English, French, Danish, Dutch and the Jewish form of Spanish known as Ladino. Very probably, England has not been a monolingual country at all since the occupation of the originally Welsh-speaking country by the Latin-speaking Romans.

There is also one other indigenous language that we must mention. This is British Sign Language, the language used (although of course not spoken) by the deaf community in this country. It has gradually come to be recognized that this is a genuine language in its own right, with its own structures and expressive power, and that it does not bear a particularly close relationship to English. Like other minority languages, it has had a history of persecution at the hands of people who have believed that it was not a 'proper' means of communication and that the deaf would be better employed trying to learn English. But it is undoubtedly a rich and subtle means of communication for those who are congenitally deaf and without it their lives would be much the poorer.

British Sign Language has recognizable regional dialects, with small differences in the signs used in different parts of the country. We shall nevertheless not be discussing BSL in the rest of this book. Nor shall we be discussing the other languages of England, whether, like Cornish, they arrived here before English or, like Panjabi, they arrived after. This is a book about English, and we shall be looking only at dialects of English in England. We shall, however, acknowledge the debt that English owes to the other languages in its vocabulary. We will also be saying that England would be a poorer place without its rich pattern of regional dialects. The same is equally true of the rich pattern of different languages that characterizes England in the late twentieth century.

2

◆

The Pronunciation of Traditional Dialects

If we want to find out where a speaker of Traditional Dialect comes from, there are a number of clues we can look for in their pronunciation. In this chapter, we will look at some of these pronunciation features and try to build up a broad outline picture of how the older, mostly rural dialects of England differ from one another, as well as from the more Modern Dialects.

Features of Traditional Dialects

LONG: 'LANG' VS 'LONG'

One of the most striking differences between Traditional Dialects has to do with words ending in -*ong*/-*ang*. Words such as *long, wrong, throng* are pronounced with a short 'o' /ɒ/ in most of England and in the rest of the English-speaking world. But in northern England and Scotland, words such as this have a short 'a' [a] – 'lang, wrang, thrang' – so that *long* rhymes with *bang*. The area in which *long* is pronounced 'lang' in Traditional Dialect is shown in map 1. The area involved includes northern Yorkshire and Lancashire, Cumbria, Durham and Northumberland. This is a very ancient dialect difference indeed, going back to the Old English period more than 1,000 years ago. The pronunciation with 'a' is the original pronunciation, and became changed to 'o' in the south of England during the course of the Old English period. *Lang* is still the word for 'long' in Dutch, German, Danish and Norwegian as well as in northern Britain

Most English people are familiar with the 'lang' pronunciation as a feature of Scottish dialects, as for example in the well-known song by Robert Burns 'Auld Lang Syne' = 'old long ago':

20

Map 1 *Long*

For auld lang syne, my jo,
For auld lang syne,
We'll tak a cup o' kindness yet
For auld lang syne.[1]

As the map shows, however, this pronunciation is as much a part of
English Traditional Dialects north of the river Humber as it is of Scots.
This can be seen in some Traditional Dialect poetry from Cumberland.
Note the spelling of *long* and *wrong*:

21

How lang I've fasted, and 'til hardly four;
This day I doubt 'ill ne'er be gitten owr,
And theer as lang a night, aleis! beside:
I lall thought fasts seck fearful things to bide.

Fie, Roger, fie! a sairy lass to wrang,
And let her aw this trouble undergang.[2]

(Here *lall* means 'little' and *sairy* means 'poor'.)

Personal surnames such as Lang or Laing and Strang are northern versions of the southern names Long and Strong, and there are many northern place names which also show this form, such as Langdale = 'long valley' in Cumbria and Langcliffe = 'long cliff' in Yorkshire. (Place-names in the south such as Langham, Norfolk, date from the earlier Old English period before the sound change took place.)

NIGHT: 'NEET' VS 'NITE'

Words such as *right, light, night* are pronounced 'rite, nite' /raɪt, naɪt/ in most parts of England, but in quite a large area in the north they have an older pronunciation 'reet, neet' /riːt, niːt/. Map 2 shows that this area is not identical with the 'lang' area, but does include Yorkshire and the far north. In this case also, the difference between the northern area and the southern area has arisen because the newer 'rite' /raɪt/ pronunciation, which has been developing and spreading northwards from the south of England for the last several centuries, has not yet reached the northern area of England. As with the 'lang, strang' pronunciations we have just discussed, the northern part of the country is more conservative in its pronunciation than the south. (Scottish dialects have an even older pronunciation, the original Anglo-Saxon 'richt' /rɪxt/.)

Forms of this type can be noted in the following verses from the Wearside (Sunderland) area of the northeast, where *right, night* and *frighten* are rendered as 'reet', 'neet' and 'freeten'. Note also *long* and *song* as 'lang' and 'sang'. (Other words: *wee* = 'who', *tiv* = 'to'.)

Mark Fortin' at steeith had just moor'd his keel,
An' the neet was that dark it wad freeten the deil;
Ye could not see yer thumb eff ye held up yer hand,
When Mark started off for ti come ower land.

22

Map 2 *Night*

He call'd at the Reed Dog, but he didn't stay lang,
Smok'd his pipe, had some talk, an' sung a bit sang;
He'd had nowt ti drink for ti mak' him feel queer –
On'y two pots o' rum and three quairts o' beer.

As he cam' on past Painshaw it cam' on ti blaw,
An' his shoe sole cam' lowse, but poor Mark didn't knaw,
An' as he kept walkin' it flopp' div ye see,
Sayin' 'Click'em and catch'em' as plain as could be.

23

His hair it stood up wiv the fright an' the fear,
An' he durstn't luck round for ti see wee was near;
But he set off ti run at a bonny round pace,
As if life an' death did depend on the race.

But the faster he ran, tiv his horror and pain,
The quicker the shoe gav' the dridful refrain;
For 'Click'em and catch'em' was dinn'd in his ear,
Till he felt he was likely ti drop down wi' fear.

Tiv Offerton he ran, his heart pitty-pat,
Reet intiv the Inn, like a weel-scadded cat,
His breath was maist gyen, but he just mey'd a mint,
Cryin' 'Shut tee the door, there's the auld man behint!'[3]

*B*LIND: 'BLINND' VS 'BLINED'

Here again we find a very ancient difference between English dialects. In the Anglo-Saxon language, in words containing *-ind* such as *blind* and *find*, the *i* was pronounced short. More than a thousand years ago, this was lengthened before *nd* to give the modern 'blined' /blaɪnd/ pronunciation in most of England. But this change never occurred in the area of central and northern England, shown in map 3, where 'finnd' /fɪnd/ and 'blinnd' /blɪnd/ still occur in Traditional Dialect. It is clearly not too much of an exaggeration to say that the Traditional Dialects of northern England are generally more conservative as far as pronunciation is concerned than those of the south. They have simply changed rather less since Anglo-Saxon times than southern dialects.

*L*AND: 'LAND' VS 'LOND'

Yet another dialect difference of great antiquity involves the pronunciation of words like *land, hand, man*. In Anglo-Saxon times, there developed a strong tendency in certain areas of England to change a short 'a' to a short 'o' in words where the vowel occurred in front of an *n*. Thus 'land' became 'lond' /lɒnd/ just as 'lang' became 'long'. However, this change was much less successful than the 'lang' to 'long' change, and took root only in western areas of the country. As map 4 shows, this difference has persisted for perhaps twelve centuries or so

24

Map 3   *Blind*

and still distinguishes between dialects in the west, from Lancashire down to Herefordshire, with 'o', and dialects to the east, with 'a'.

ARM: 'ARRM' VS 'AHM'

A more recent dialect feature that will probably be known to most people involves the way in which speakers say words like *arm, cart, far*. Originally, all dialects of English used to pronounce all *r*s, wherever

25

Map 4   *Land*

they occurred in a word. Starting around 250 years ago or so, however, in some dialects 'r' started to be dropped where it occurred before a consonant, as in *arm*, or before a pause, as in *far*. Where *r* occurred before a vowel, as in *rack, track, carry*, however, it was retained. In those parts of the country where 'r' was dropped, words like *tar* and *ta*, *mar* and *ma* were now pronounced the same. In other areas with the original pronunciation, pairs like this continued to be distinguished by the presence or absence of 'r'.

26

Map 5   *Arm*; r = *r* pronounced in *arm* etc.; (r) = some *r*s pronounced

Note that when we talk of dialects which do not have an 'r' in words like *cart*, we are talking about the pronunciation and not the spelling. Dropping the 'r' in *cart* does not turn it into *cat*. It simply means that *cart* is pronounced 'caht' /kaːt/ rather than the original 'carrt' /kaːrt/.

As far as we can tell, this change appears to have started in the southeast of England and to have spread subsequently to other parts of the country. Map 5 shows the parts of England in which 'r' is retained in Traditional Dialects in words like *cart* and *arm*. Note that some areas

27

such as eastern Yorkshire are indicated as having *partial* retention of 'r'. This simply means that 'r' is retained in certain words or positions but not in others. It is clear even from the map that the pronunciation without 'r' is a newer pronunciation which has gradually spread north and west, cutting originally *r*-pronouncing areas off from one another. Here it has been the east of England which has been innovating, with the west and far north remaining more conservative.

Because rural areas close to London were among those which retained the 'r', pronunciations such as 'ferrtilizerr' [fəːɹdəlɔɪzəɹ] and 'manurre' [mənjuəɹ] are often used by urban speakers in the south of England to mock country people for being unsophisticated peasants. Americans, on the other hand, are not mocked in this way, even though most of them pronounce their *r*s in *cart* and *arm*, and indeed in most parts of the United States saying 'ferrdilizerr' [fəːɹdəlaɪzəɹ] is considered to be a pronunciation superior to the pronunciation without the 'r's. The fact is that in England omitting 'r's in words such as these is a feature of educated speech, and is therefore not stigmatized as being undesirable. No one is criticized for 'dropping' their 'r's as they are for 'dropping' their 'h's (see the following section).

HILL: 'HILL' VS 'ILL'

All dialects of English used to pronounce the consonant 'h' in words such as *hit* and *house*. This consonant, however, is not a particularly useful one in English, since it can only occur (in pronunciation) at the beginning of a word, as in *hit*, or at the beginning of a stressed syllable, as in *behind*. There are no words in English in which 'h' is pronounced before a consonant or at the end of the word. If we compare 'h' with 'l', for example, we can see that 'l' is a much more useful consonant which can occur in many different positions in a word: *lit, flit, silly, silk, sill*. By contrast, although we do have words such as *hit* in English, there are no words – and could not be any words – like **fhit, *sihhy, *sihk, *sihh*.

Perhaps because 'h' is therefore a relatively unimportant consonant in English, very many– in fact most – local dialects in England have lost this consonant altogether over the last few hundred years. (The same development has also taken place in French and Italian, with for instance the original 'h' of Latin *hominem* 'man' not being pronounced in modern French *homme* or Italian *uomo*). This means that most local dialects have 'ouse' /aus/ and 'ammer' /æmə/ rather than 'house'

28

Map 6   *Hill:* 'hill' vs 'ill'

/haʊs/ and 'hammer' /hæmə/, so that the pairs *hill* and *ill, ham* and *am, heart* and *art* are pronounced the same. In a normal sentence, this is most unlikely to give rise to any misunderstandings, and it is not something to be deplored any more than the loss of 'r' discussed above, which has led to, for example, *arms* and *alms, lore* and *law* being pronounced the same.

Map 6 shows that Traditional Dialects in two geographically periph-eral parts of the country, the northeast and East Anglia, have not shared in this change. They have remained more conservative in this respect than the rest of the country, because the change has not yet reached these areas. Scotland and Ireland, too, remain *h*-pronouncing areas.

SEVEN: 'SEVEN' VS 'ZEVEN'

In the Middle Ages an interesting pronunciation change took place in most of the dialects along the south coast of England from Kent to Devon. In this change, the consonants 'f', 's', 'sh' /f, s, ʃ/ at the beginning of words became 'v', 'z', 'zh' /v, z, ʒ/, giving pronunciations such as 'zeven zhillings and vorpence' /zevn ʒɪlɪŋz n vɔːrpəns/. A few words from these south-coast dialects even made their way further north. This is why we have a male *fox* but a female *vixen* – 'vixen' was originally a southern dialect form with the original 'f' changed to 'v'.

In modern times, the area of England in which Traditional Dialects have this feature has become rather smaller, as is shown in map 7: Kent and Sussex, for example, no longer have this feature. It can be seen, though, that dialect speakers in Somerset still call their county 'Zummerzet', and the pronunciation also still occurs in Devon, Dorset, and parts of Cornwall, Gloucestershire, Wiltshire and Hampshire. A recent Wiltshire dialect poem, for instance, goes:

> When I were jus' a leetle bwoy
> I met an old man in tha street,
> Ee zeemed ta be quite pleasent enuff
> 'Is chat an' 'is zmyle wer zweet.
>
> But I 'membered wot me mum 'ad zed,
> 'Never ta ztop an' talk to a stranger',
> But 'ee zeemed ta knaw wot I wer thinking,
> 'Coz 'ee zed, 'My bwoy, ther is noa danger.'
>
> Then 'ee put iz hand on my yarm,
> Az a zmyle 'cross 'iz face did zet,
> Zaying, 'Ther's noa zich thing az strangers;
> Ther only vrends you 'aven't met.'[4]

We can say that the south of England was an innovating dialect area as far as this change is concerned, but that the innovation has not, in

Map 7 *Seven*

the very long run, been particularly successful and will probably eventually die out again, with the original 'f-', 's-' and 'sh-' forms gradually returning.

BAT: 'BĂT' VS 'BÆT' [BAT] VS [BÆT]

Our final feature is of rather more recent origin, having begun life in the southeast of England probably no more than 200 years ago. This

Map 8   *Bat*

involves the short 'a' vowel of words like *bat*, *bad*, *man*, etc. The innovation that occurred in the case of the southeastern dialects was that the 'a' vowel acquired the 'clear' [æ] pronunciation that it has today in BBC English, while the north of England, as is well known, retained the original 'flat' 'ă' [a] pronunciation, so that a northerner saying 'bat' sounds a little bit like a southerner saying *but* or 'baht'. To a northerner, on the other hand, southerners saying *bat* sound almost as if they are saying *bet*. Map 8 shows the 'băt' or 'baht' type pronunciation is also used in the southwest of England. In this book, when we want to refer specifically to the southeastern/BBC way of saying 'a', we will use the letter æ corresponding to the phonetic symbol [æ].

The Overall Picture

These, then, are the eight major features of English Traditional Dialects which we can use to divide the country up into different dialect areas, thus helping us to recognize where dialect speakers come from:

	older form		newer form	
long	lang	/læŋ/	long	/lɒŋ/
night	neet	/niːt/	nite	/naɪt/
blind	blinnd	/blɪnd/	blined	/blaɪnd/
land	land	/lænd/	lond	/lɒnd/
arm	arrm	/aːrm/	ahm	/aːm/
hill	hill	/hɪl/	ill	/ɪl/
seven	seven	/sevn/	zeven	/zevn/
bat	băt	[bat]	bæt	[bæt]

If we combine maps 1–8 into a composite map, this gives us the picture we present here in map 9. The map shows that England can be divided up into thirteen different Traditional Dialect areas. Excluded from this subdivision in map 9 are those areas of the country

Table 2.1

	Long	Night	Blind	Land	Arm	Hill	Seven	Bat
Northumberland	lang	neet	blinnd	land	arrm	hill	seven	bat
Lower North	lang	neet	blinnd	land	ahm	ill	seven	bat
Lancashire	long	neet	blined	lond	arrm	ill	seven	bat
Staffordshire	long	nite	blined	lond	ahm	ill	seven	bat
South Yorkshire	long	neet	blinnd	land	ahm	ill	seven	bat
Lincolnshire	long	nite	blinnd	land	ahm	ill	seven	bat
Leicestershire	long	nite	blined	land	ahm	ill	seven	bat
Western Southwest	long	nite	blined	land	arrm	ill	zeven	bat
Northern Southwest	long	nite	blined	lond	arrm	ill	seven	bat
Eastern Southwest	long	nite	blined	land	arrm	ill	seven	bat
Southeast	long	nite	blined	lænd	arrm	ill	seven	bæt
Central East	long	nite	blined	lænd	ahm	ill	seven	bæt
Eastern Counties	long	nite	blined	lænd	ahm	hill	seven	bæt

Map 9   Traditional Dialect areas

which were not English-speaking until the eighteenth century or later
and where Traditional Dialects have not therefore had time to develop:
western Cornwall and most of Wales. Also excluded is the urban area
of London – for a discussion of Cockney see pp. 46–7. The thirteen
areas, and their pronunciations of the eight features, are given in
table 2.1.

It will be seen that in map 9 we have not only divided the country

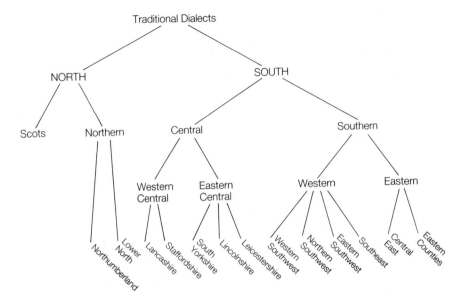

Figure 2.1

up into thirteen dialect areas. We have also marked some of the boundaries between the dialect areas as being more significant than others. In fact, the different importance given to the boundaries is intended to indicate a grouping of dialects, based on differences and similarities between them, as shown also in figure 2.1.

Both map 9 and figure 2.1 show that the major division of English Traditional Dialects is into dialects of the NORTH and dialects of the SOUTH, and that the boundary between them runs from the Lancashire coast down to the mouth of the River Humber. This is the most important Traditional Dialect boundary in Britain. The dialects of Scotland and the far north of England thus form one major group of English dialects, with the dialects of the rest of England forming the other.

As far as England itself is concerned, the NORTH dialect area includes Northumberland, Durham, Cumbria, northern Yorkshire, and the far north of Lancashire. It is astonishing to realize that this major dialect boundary still follows, up to a point, the Anglo–Saxon dialect boundary between the old kingdoms of Northumbria and Mercia, which in turn may even reflect, although this is by no means certain, the Anglo–Saxon Europe-to-Britain settlement patterns – see map 10.

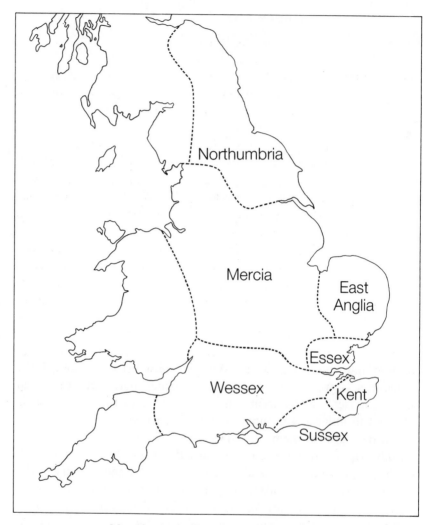

Map 10   Anglo-Saxon kingdoms c.AD 650

Our reason for placing the primary English dialect boundary here is that the *long*: 'lang' vs 'long' boundary, which it follows, is by no means the only dialect boundary to follow this route. Along this line is where we find the boundary between many other important dialect features within English Traditional Dialects. We can briefly discuss some of them.

The North

Some of the important features, in addition to the 'lang, wrang' pronunciation that we have already mentioned, which distinguish the NORTH dialect area from the SOUTH, are the following:

1   Words such as *house*, *out* and *cow* are pronounced 'hoose' /huːs/, 'oot' /uːt/ and 'coo' /kuː/ in the NORTH. In the Traditional Dialects of Scotland and the far north of England, the original mediaeval pronunciation of these sorts of words – with a pure vowel – has been retained, while from late mediaeval times onwards the southern part of the country has gradually acquired the 'ow' /aʊ/ diphthong. (A **diphthong** is a vowel which changes its quality from beginning to end, like 'oi' in *boil*, whereas a **monophthong** is a pure vowel which remains the same throughout its pronunciation, like 'ah' in *calm*.) Most of us are familiar with this pronunciation from stereotypical Scots phrases such as 'there's a moose loose aboot the hoose', but it is found in Traditional Dialects in northern England also. Indeed, this particular feature actually extends just over the river Humber into northern Lincolnshire (which comes into our South Yorkshire dialect area). This can be seen (in the words *down*, *round*, *out*, *doubt*) in an extract from the poem 'The Lincolnshire Poacher' (note also the pronunciation of *moonlight night*):

> Bud I'd rayther be doon wheare th'fire
> An' brimstun foriver bo'ns,
> An' just goä roond wi' a bucket
> An' give fook drink by to'ns –
> Then sit i' yon stright maade heaven,
> Wheare saints an' aängels sing,
> An' niver hear a pheasant craw,
> Nor th'skirr o' a partridge wing;
> Wheare ther' isn't a bank nor a plantin'-side
> Wheare rabbits cum oot an' plaay,
> An' stamp wi' ther' feet o' a moonleet neet,
> Wheare it's warm o' th' coudest daay;[5]

2   Words such as *home*, *bone* and *stone* originally, in Anglo-Saxon, had an 'a' vowel. In the case of the word *home*, this can still be seen in the

word *hamlet*, and in the spelling of very many English placenames which end in *-ham* with the original meaning 'home of': Buckingham, Nottingham, Grantham, Hailsham, etc. In late Anglo-Saxon or early mediaeval times, this 'a' vowel changed in pronunciation to a long 'o' in England south of the Humber, giving the modern 'home' pronunciation.

In the conservative area north of the Humber, this change did not take place. As a result, today Scots dialects have the same long 'ā' vowel in *stone* [steːn] and *home* [heːm] that they do in *name* [neːm]: 'stane', 'hame'. In the Burns poem 'O'er the Water to Charlie', for instance, we find

> I lo'e weel my Charlie's name,
> Tho' some there be abhor him:
> But O, to see auld Nick gaun hame,
> And Charlie's faes before him![6]

(Here *faes* means 'foes'.) In the NORTH of England the same failure to change Anglo-Saxon 'a' to 'o' is found, but Traditional Dialects here have a vowel that is usually of the type 'ee-a' or 'ay-a' in words such as this: *home* 'hee-am' [hɪem], *stone* 'stee-an' [stɪen].

3   Finally, dialects of the NORTH typically do not have the long 'oo' vowel that SOUTH dialects have in words such as *fool, spoon, boot*. Instead, they have a diphthong of the type 'ee-oo' or 'ee-a', as in 'spee-oon' [spɪʊn ~ spɪən] for spoon.

Typical NORTH pronunciations are thus:

the *wrong spoon*	[ðə raŋ spɪʊn]	'the rang spee-oon'
a *stone house*	[ə stɪen huːs]	'a stee-an hoose'

SUBDIVISIONS

These features, then, would help us decide that a dialect speaker came from somewhere north of the Humber. Obviously, however, we need to look at more features if we want to narrow down speakers' origins more closely. If we try to distinguish smaller, more narrowly based dialect areas, we find that, not surprisingly perhaps in view of the national border, the major division within the NORTH is between **Scots** dialects, on the one hand, and those of the English part of the NORTH, which we will here call **Northern**, on the other. **Scots** dialects have very many features of their own. For example, as we have seen, they do not have the 'neet' /niːt/ pronunciation of *night* that we discussed above, but rather an even older pronunciation, 'nicht' /nɪxt/, as in 'a braw bricht moonlicht nicht', which is not now found anywhere in England, although the 'ch' sound of Scots *loch* or German *Nacht* could certainly be found, if with difficulty, in words such as *enough* in parts of Lancashire and Yorkshire until recently, and was even found in the urban speech of Huddersfield in the early years of this century. We will not be dealing further with dialects of Scots in this book.

Northern Dialects

Within the Northern (i.e. English) area of the NORTH, we make a further subdivision, as map 9 and figure 2.1 show. These two subdivisions of the Northern area we call the **Northumberland** and **Lower North** dialect areas.

Northumberland   The Northumberland area, which also includes some adjacent areas of Cumbria and Durham, has a number of distinctive features of pronunciation which would help us recognize speakers as coming from there. It is the only area of England, for example, to retain the Anglo-Saxon and mediaeval distinction between words like *witch* and *which* as 'witch' and 'hwitch'. Elsewhere in the country, the 'hw' sound has been lost and replaced by 'w' so that *whales* is identical with *Wales*, *what* with *watt*, and so on. This distinction also survives in Scotland, Ireland and parts of North America and New Zealand, but as far as the natural vernacular speech of England is concerned, Northumberland is uniquely conservative in retaining 'hw'. This means that in Northumberland, trade names like *Weetabix* don't work very well since *weet* suggests 'weet' /wiːt/ whereas *wheat* is locally pronounced 'hweet' /hwiːt/.

Northumberland also retains the consonant 'h' in *hill* etc., as we saw in map 6, and has a very distinctive pronunciation [R] of 'r' which is known as the 'Northumbrian burr'. This means that 'r' is pronounced with the back of the tongue rather than the tip. Technically, the 'r' is produced by moving the back of the tongue towards the uvula, as in French and German.

The Lower North   The dialects of the Lower North differ from those

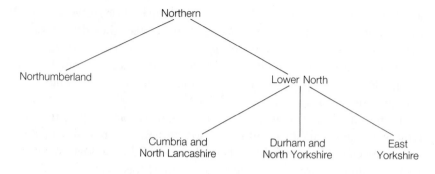

Figure 2.2

of Northumberland by not having 'h', 'hw' or the 'Northumbrian burr'. Lower North dialects are spoken in most of Cumbria and the Lake District, most of county Durham, the far north of Lancashire, and northern and eastern Yorkshire. This is a rather large area which can be further subdivided (see figure 2.2), if we like, as follows:

(a) Cumbria and North Lancashire
(b) Durham and North Yorkshire
(c) East Yorkshire.

Amongst other criteria, areas (a) and (c) differ from (b) in pronouncing 'r' in some words, but not all, before a consonant. For example, East Yorkshire dialect has kept 'r' after the 'er' /ɜː/ vowel in words like *bird* and *first*, while Cumbria has it in words like *hare* and *bare* (see map 5).

So, if we notice that a Traditional Dialect speaker says, for example, 'lang' for *long*, we know that they come from the north dialect area. If we want to discover more exactly where they come from, we can use the following diagnostic words (*R* stands for the back-of-the-tongue pronunciation of *r* – the 'Northumbrian burr'):

	night	*hill*	*which*	*hare*	*first*
Scotland	nicht	h	hw	r	r
Northumberland	neet	h	hw	R	R
Cumbria	neet	–	w	r	–
Durham and North Yorks.	neet	–	w	–	–
East Yorkshire	neet	–	w	–	r

Of course, each of these dialects has many other distinguishing characteristics as well, and each area could be subdivided further and further, even right down to individual villages, in some cases. We do not have the space to do this here, however.

The South

The SOUTH Traditional Dialect area covers all the areas of England south of the Humber, except western Cornwall, and also includes those areas of eastern Wales which are English Traditional Dialect-speaking.

As can be seen from figure 2.1 and map 9, the SOUTH is divided, like the NORTH, into two major areas. We call these major areas the **Central and Southern** dialect areas. In terms of the eight criteria we used for establishing dialect areas, the boundary between Central and Southern dialects coincides with the *bat*: 'băt' [a] vs 'bæt' [æ] boundary in the east, and with the *arm*: 'arrm' /aːrm/ vs 'ahm' /aːm/ boundary in the west. Obviously these features are not enough on their own to justify the setting up of a major dialect boundary. We place it here because this boundary also coincides, approximately, with the boundaries for a number of other important features.

In particular, it coincides with the well-known dialect difference that concerns the pronunciation of words such as *past, laugh, path*. Here again is a feature where a more southerly area is more innovating than the area to its north. Until about 200 years ago, all dialects of English had a short 'a' vowel in all words of this type, but then a change began in which 'ă' [a] became lengthened to 'ah' [aː] before 's', 'f' and 'th' /s, f, θ/, as in *glass, chaff, bath*. This change was very successful in the Southern dialect area, but never made it north of the line which crosses England from Wales to the Wash, and thus distinguishes between Southern and Central dialects.

CENTRAL DIALECTS

The Central Traditional Dialect area covers most of Lancashire, Yorkshire and the Midlands, and is an intermediate part of the country in which, as far as dialect is concerned, we can see northern features gradually giving way to southern pronunciations as we travel south. The crucial features that we use in the subdivision of the Central area are *blind*: 'blinnd' /blind/ vs 'blined' /blaɪnd/; *night*: 'neet' /niːt/ vs

41

'nite' /naɪt/; and *land*: 'lond' /lɒnd/ vs 'land' /lænd/. They give us a division of the area as follows (see also map 9):

		Find the right man
Western:	Lancashire	'fined the reet mon'
		/faɪnd ðə riːt mɒn/
	Staffordshire	'fined the rite mon'
		/faɪnd ðə raɪt mɒn/
Eastern:	South Yorkshire	'finnd the reet man'
		/fɪnd ðə riːt man/
	Lincolnshire	'finnd the rite man'
		/fɪnd ðə raɪt man/
	Leicestershire	'fined the rite man'
		/faɪnd ðə raɪt man/

As can be seen, we use the *man*: 'mon' vs 'man' feature as the major criterion for subdividing the area into **Western Central** and **Eastern Central** parts. Note that the Leicestershire area is identical to Southern dialects in its treatment of these three features.

Western Central   Geographically, the **Lancashire** area covers Lancashire itself, apart from the far north, plus neighbouring areas of northeastern Cheshire and northwestern Derbyshire. In addition to the features we have just mentioned, the Lancashire dialects also pronounce the *r* in *arm* etc. (see map 5).

The **Staffordshire** dialect area includes the whole of Staffordshire itself plus most of Cheshire, northern Shropshire, and parts of southern Derbyshire, northwestern Warwickshire and northeastern Worcestershire. Large parts of this area, including the Potteries, have an interesting system of Traditional Dialect vowel sounds which make the dialect distinctively different from the areas around it. Thus:

> *bait* is pronounced like *beat*
> *beat* is pronounced like *bait*
> *bought* is pronounced like *boat*
> *boat* is pronounced like *boot*
> *boot* is pronounced like *bout*
> *bout* is pronounced like *bite*
> *bite* is pronounced like 'baht' [baːt]

In this dialect, *it seems the same* is pronounced 'it sames the seem'.

Eastern Central The **South Yorkshire** dialect area is a large region comprising southern and western Yorkshire, northern Lincolnshire, northern Nottinghamshire, and northeastern Derbyshire. This area is characterized, in addition to the other features we have mentioned, by a pronunciation of words such as *home, bone, stone* with a vowel of the type 'oo-a' [ʊə], so that *stone* is pronounced 'stoo-an' [stʊən].

The **Lincolnshire** Dialect area consists of only central Lincolnshire, while the **Leicestershire** area includes Leicestershire plus south Nottinghamshire and parts of western Lincolnshire.

SOUTHERN DIALECTS

This Traditional Dialect area covers the whole of the south of England, from the Wash to the Bristol Channel, but includes also those areas which lie north of the Bristol Channel and west of the West Midlands as far as Shrewsbury, together with the adjacent areas of Wales.

We divide this part of the country into six major dialect areas, using the criteria based on *land, arm, hill, bat* and *seven* as follows:

	arm	*land*	*seven*	*bat*	*hill*
Western:					
Western Southwest	arrm	hand	zeven	bat	ill
Northern Southwest	arrm	hond	seven	bat	ill
Eastern Southwest	arrm	hand	seven	bat	ill
Southeast	arrm	hænd	seven	bæt	ill
Eastern:					
Central East	ahm	hænd	seven	bæt	ill
Eastern Counties	ahm	hænd	seven	bæt	hill

Western Dialects Here we have used the presence or absence of 'r' in *arm* as the major distinction between Western and Eastern dialects within the Southern area. As far as Western dialects are concerned, the **Western Southwest** consists geographically of Cornwall, Devon, Somerset, Wiltshire and Dorset, plus southern Gloucestershire and southwestern Hampshire. The **Northern Southwest** consists of south Shropshire, Herefordshire, east Monmouth and west Worcestershire, while the **Eastern Southwest** includes Oxfordshire, western Bucking-

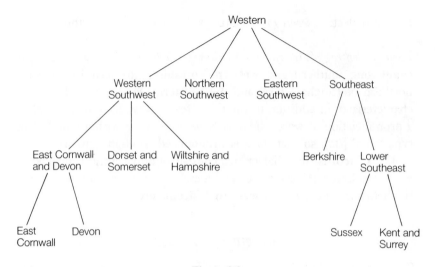

Figure 2.3

hamshire, north Gloucestershire and south Warwickshire. The **Southeast** area covers Berkshire, northeastern Hampshire, Sussex, Surrey and Kent.

Both the Southeast and the Western Southwest areas are very large, and it is possible to divide them up further if we are trying to decide where a dialect speaker comes from. This additional subdivision is shown in figure 2.3.

Distinguishing features within the **Western Southwest** include:

1 the insertion of 'w' before 'o' in words like *old* 'word' and *boil* 'bwile';
2 the pronunciation of *t* in words like *better*, *city* as 'd' – 'ciddy';
3 the pronunciation of the vowel of words like *boot*, *rude* with a very front '*ü*' vowel [yː] like the *u* of French or the *ü* of German.

This gives us:

	boot	*city*	*old*
East Cornwall	boot	ciddy	old
Devon	büüt	ciddy	old
Dorset and Somerset	boot	ciddy	wold
Wiltshire and Hampshire	boot	city	old

Distinguishing features within the **Southeast** dialect area include:

1   the loss of 'l' at the end of words like *school* and *fool*;
2   the pronunciation of *o* in words like *old*, *cold* with a diphthong [au] almost like 'ow' in *now*.

This gives us:

	school	*old*
Berkshire	school	old
Sussex	schoo	owld
Kent and Surrey	school	owld

Eastern Dialects   If we turn now to Eastern dialects within the Southern area, that is those dialects which do not have 'r' in *arm*, we see that there are two major sub-areas, the **Central East** and the **Eastern Counties** dialect areas. The Eastern Counties area consists of Norfolk, Suffolk and northeastern Essex. As we have seen, Eastern Counties Traditional Dialect is characterized by the retention of 'h'. It is also notable for the pronunciation of words like *stone*, *home*, *road* with the same short vowel as in *put*, *pull*, so that *road* /rʊd/ rhymes with *good* and *goat* /gʊt/ rhymes with *put*. A Norfolk dialect poet has written, in 'The Tawny Owl':

> Yew poor ole feller, by some car cut down
> As over that there wall yew come laast night,
> A-layin' dead there on the frorsty ground,
> Them gret eyes wide, that sharp ole beak shet tight.
>
> No more yew 'oon't fly up and down this rood,
> Wi' baads a-scoldin' yew on evra side;
> No more yew 'oon't go in an' out the wood,
> T'saach where all them little creatures hide.[7]

Here the word *road*, spelt 'rood' /rʊd/, rhymes with *wood*.

The **Central East** area includes most of the central and eastern parts of Northamptonshire, together with Cambridgeshire, eastern Buckinghamshire, and non-metropolitan Hertfordshire and Essex (apart from the northeast). This dialect area is probably one of the least known of all English dialect areas in the sense that few English people have preconceived ideas or stereotypes of what the dialect is like. This is probably because this dialect is the most innovative of all the areas we have set up. Of the eight pronunciation features we have used, the Central East has the newer variant in seven cases:

long	'long'	/lɒŋ/
night	'nite'	/naɪt/
blind	'blined'	/blaɪnd/
land	'lænd'	/lænd/
arm	'ahm'	/aːm/
hill	'ill'	/ɪl/
bat	'bæt'	/bæt/

The only feature in which it does not have the newer form is *seven*: 'zeven', and as we have seen, this 'innovation' is actually fast dying out. The central geographical position of this dialect tends to stress its neutral character, and it is also linguistically quite close to the standard language, which historically grew out of dialects in this area.

The **Central East** can be further subdivided, if we wish, into two smaller units, as shown in figure 2.4. Features of relevance here include:

1 the pronunciation of -*ing* (see below);
2 the loss of 'l' at the end of words.

This gives us:

	arm	*hill*	*school*
Eastern Counties	ahm	hill	school
Northamptonshire and Cambridgeshire	ahm	ill	school
Essex	ahm	ill	schoo

We should also include in this area some discussion of **Cockney**, the Traditional Dialect of working-class London. It is arguable whether modern Cockney contains any elements of Traditional Dialect at all, or whether it should be considered only under the heading of Modern Dialects. Nineteenth-century Cockney certainly was a Traditional Dialect, however, and would have to be considered as having been a separate branch of the Eastern dialects (it pronounces *arm* as 'ahm', for

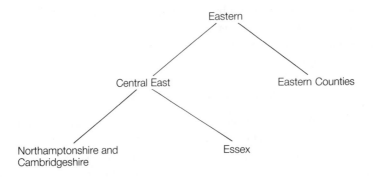

Figure 2.4

instance) in addition to the Eastern Counties and the Central East. The following extract from a nineteenth-century song by George Le Brunn shows not only features still typical of modern Cockney such as *town* as [tæːn] 'tahn' and *think* as 'fink', but also *vex* as 'wex'. This *w* instead of *v* is clearly a feature of Traditional Dialect, and no longer occurs in London English, but it did survive in other Eastern dialects until recently – many people in the Eastern Counties still remember hearing their grandparents saying *victuals* 'wittals' and *village* 'willage' – and of course Dickens's character Sam Weller is also famous for having had this pronunciation.

> I've lost my pal, 'e's the best in all the tahn,
> But don't you fink 'im dead, becos 'e ain't.
> But since he's wed, 'e 'as ter nuckle dahn,
> It's enough ter wex the temper of a saint.
> 'E's a brewer's drayman, wiv a leg of mutton fist,
> An' as strong as a bullick or an horse.
> Yet in 'er 'ands 'e's like a little kid,
> Oh! I wish as I could get him a divorce.[8]

Further Important Dialect Features

There is so much variety in the pronunciation of English dialects that we could actually fill several books on the topic. We have had to confine ourselves here to a small number of features of pronunciation, and to quite large dialect areas. There are, however, two further

47

features we should mention which can help to localize speakers further, and which, interestingly enough, cut across some of the major dialect areas we have already set up.

Walking: 'WALKINN' VS 'WALK'N'

The first of these concerns the way in which dialect speakers pronounce -*ing* at the end of words such as *walking*, *running*, *going*, etc. In some areas this suffix is pronounced 'inn' to give 'walkinn' /wɔːkɪn/, while in others it is pronounced 'n' to give 'walk'n' /wɔːkən/. The different dialect areas treat -*ing* as follows:

'walkinn'	'walk'n'
Durham and North Yorkshire	Northumberland
East Yorkshire	Cumbria
Central	Devon and East Cornwall
Wiltshire and Hampshire	Somerset and Dorset
Eastern Southwest	Eastern Counties
Northern Southwest	Essex
Southeast	
Central East	

This means that '-inn' occurs in all the central areas of England, with '-n' confined to the peripheral areas of the north, the southwestern peninsula, and the Eastern Counties and Essex.

Moan/*mown* – SAME VS DIFFERENT

The second feature has to do with the number of vowels a dialect has. Does the dialect have the same vowel in *moan* as in *mown*? We can distinguish in English spelling between two sets of words:

oa/ *o-e*	*ow*/ *ou*
moan	mown
road	rowed
nose	knows
sole	soul
rose	rows
toe	tow etc.

Words like this are spelt differently because, in late mediaeval times when English spelling was beginning to be established, they were pronounced differently by all English speakers. Words with *oa* or *o-e* had a monophthong or pure vowel, perhaps rather like 'aw' [ɔː], while the words spelt with *ow/ou* had a diphthong. In most modern forms of English around the world, this distinction has been lost, including in the BBC accent, so that these pairs of words are pronounced the same. In many Traditional Dialects in England, however, the old distinction has remained. Again, those that have the older system with the extra vowel are mostly in the north or towards the geographical edge of the country:

moan/mown the same	*moan/mown* different
Leicestershire	NORTH
Central East	Western Central
Southeast	South Yorkshire
Dorset and Somerset	Lincolnshire
East Cornwall and Devon	Eastern Counties
	Eastern Southwest
	Wiltshire and Hampshire

In the dialects of the Eastern Counties, for instance, *moan* and *mown* are distinguished as 'moon' [muːn] and 'mown' [mʌun], and in all these areas puns such as IOU = 'I owe you' and 'Rubber Soul' = 'rubber sole' do not work because *owe* and *O*, *soul* and *sole* are pronounced differently.

Localizing Dialects

It should now be possible, given a local Traditional Dialect speaker or text, to localize them fairly accurately. Here is an example from modern dialect poetry:

Me 'usband came whome tother night,
An' put a card on the table;
Zo I picked un up an' read the words,
'Come to a Christmas paartee if yer able'

'Twas vrom the Squire, me 'usband's boss;
Zo I zaid, 'Well, be we gwoing?'

49

'Gwoing!' he zaid, 'I should 'ope zo,
'Twill be a change from milking an' zowing.'[9]

This is quite easily localizable. Forms such as *zo, vrom, zaid, zowing* place the origins of this poem very clearly in the Western Southwest area, while the forms *whome* and *gwoing* indicate an origin in the Somerset and Dorset sub-area (the writer is in fact from Dorset).

Suppose now that you heard a Traditional Dialect speaker say:

'Time to set out – it's ten past. It's not far – about half a mile.'

If you were lucky, that might be enough for you to pinpoint him or her fairly accurately, to within forty miles, say. Suppose the speaker's pronunciation was like this:

pronunciation	*conclusion*
time to set *owt*	not NORTH ('oot') – must be SOUTH
's ten *pahst*	not Central ('păsst') – must be Southern
's not *fah*	not Western ('farr') – must be Eastern
'bout *half* a mile	not Central East ('alf') – must be Eastern Counties

The speaker, you can conclude, is from somewhere in Norfolk, Suffolk or northeast Essex.

Let's take another example. Suppose you hear a Traditional Dialect speaker say:

'It won't be long – it's not far. It'll be all right – I'll give you a hand.
We'll be in by six. We'd better get home soon.'

You might then be able to work out what dialect the speaker has like this:

pronunciation	*conclusion*
it won't be *long*	not NORTH ('lang') – must be SOUTH
's not *farr*	must be Lancashire or Southwest (others: 'fah')
it'll be all *rite*	not Lancashire ('reet') – must be Southwest

I'll give you an *and*	not Northern Southwest ('ond') – must be Western or Eastern Southwest
we'll be in by *zix*	not Eastern Southwest ('six') – must be Western Southwest
we'd *bedder*	not Wiltshire/Hampshire ('better')
ged *ome*	not Somerset/Dorset ('wome') – must be Devon or East Cornwall
zoon	not Devon ('züün') – must be East Cornwall

The speaker, you can deduce, comes from somewhere in East Cornwall.

Of course, you *will* be very lucky if you get all these clues in such a short space of time. And, as we saw in chapter 1, in some parts of the country you will be quite lucky to find many Traditional Dialect speakers at all. In our next chapter, we look at some characteristics of dialect pronunciation that are rather easier to find in modern England.

3

◆

The Pronunciation of Modern Dialects

As we saw in chapter 1, most people in England no longer speak Traditional Dialect but rather some form of Modern Dialect. Modern Dialects represent more recent developments in the English language of England. Many of the features we used in chapter 2 to distinguish between Traditional Dialects cannot be used to discriminate between the Modern Dialects, because they are disappearing from the language and are not found in the speech of the majority of the population. This is true of the features we discussed in chapter 2 using the keywords *long*, *right*, *blind*, *hand*, *seven*. Pronunciations such as 'lang', 'reet', 'blinnd', 'hond', 'zeven', although of course still occurring, cannot be heard in the dialects spoken by the majority of the population of England in the last quarter of the twentieth century. The pronunciation of *hill* as 'hill' *can* still be found, but as a feature of local dialect it is dying out very rapidly in East Anglia and is really therefore a distinctive characteristic of only the northeastern region. The pronunciation of *bat* as 'bæt', on the other hand, has spread rather widely, and so is also difficult to use for characterizing Modern Dialects. This leaves *arm*: 'arrm' /aːrm/ vs 'ahm' /aːm/ as the only criterion that remains from chapter 2, although, as we shall see, the geographical area in which the pronunciation 'arrm' survives is much reduced in Modern Dialects.

If we therefore wish to locate the geographical origins of the majority of speakers in the country who are not Traditional Dialect speakers, and who do not have a BBC accent either, a number of other criteria will have to be used. The dialect areas, too, as we shall see, are often very different from the Traditional Dialect areas. The features we employ in this book to help us to distinguish between Modern Dialects are the following.

Features of Modern Dialects

THE VOWEL OF *BUT*

As everybody who has spent any time in England knows, the north and the south of England are distinguished by their pronunciation of the short *u* in words such as *but* and *up*: northerners say 'boott' /bʊt/ and 'oopp' /ʊp/, while southerners do not. Northern accents do not distinguish between pairs of words such as *could* and *cud*, or *put* and *putt*, using the short 'oo' /ʊ/ vowel throughout, while southerners use the 'oo' vowel only in *could* and *put*. Northern accents, that is, have one vowel less than southern accents, and make *but* rhyme with *put*. The reason for this is that northern accents preserve the older mediaeval or Middle English vowel system, whereas southern accents have developed the additional short *u* vowel /ʌ/ in words such as *cud* and *putt*. As we shall see below, our division of England into the two major Modern Dialect areas, North and South, is based on this feature, although we could have used others, such as the pronunciation of words like *past* (see p. 41).

We note, then, that 'oo' /ʊ/ is found in *but*-words (*cup, up, butter, some, other, luck*, etc.) in, for example, Newcastle, Bradford, Hull, Accrington, Liverpool, Manchester, Birmingham and Lincoln, whereas in places such as Bedford, Ipswich, London, Bristol and Exeter it is found only in *put*-words (*pull, butcher, wood, foot, wool, push*, etc.). See map 11 for an illustration of the areas involved.

THE PRONUNCIATION OF *R* IN *ARM*

As far as we can tell, the change of 'arrm' /aːrm/ to 'ahm' /aːm/ (see chapter 2) appears to have started in the southeast of England, especially London, the South Midlands and East Anglia, and to have spread subsequently to other parts of the country. It is certainly a change which is continuing to spread to this day. In modern urban accents there are now only two major areas of England where the older *r*-pronouncing accents strongly survive. These are in parts of Lancashire such as Blackburn and Burnley, although even here younger people seem to be losing this feature, and in the southwest of England including Cornwall, Devon, Somerset, Dorset, Gloucester, Hereford and Wiltshire. (See map 12 and compare with map 5, p. 27.) It was not

Map 11   *But*

so long ago, however, as we know from chapter 2, that most of the
south-coast rural dialects, including those of Kent, Sussex and Surrey,
were *r*-pronouncing, and the same is true of large areas of the northwest from the Lake District down to Cheshire, and of rural Northumberland, Durham and eastern Yorkshire.

Every year the *r*-pronouncing area gets smaller, and at the moment
counties like Oxfordshire, Berkshire and Hampshire appear to be in
the front line of this change, with older people retaining the 'r' in

Map 12   Areas where *r* is pronounced in *arm*

tart and younger people losing it. Towns such as Reading, Portsmouth and Southampton – and even Bournemouth – are currently in the process of losing 'r' in words of this sort. It is true that you can still hear pronunciations such as 'tarrt' /taːrt/ even in places like Guildford and Tunbridge Wells, but it does not look as if this will be true for very much longer. The process of 'r'-loss has no doubt been accelerated by the fact that this change has long since made its way into the BBC accent, so that pronouncing ones *r*s has relatively low social status in England, and omitting them relatively high social status.)

(Note that there is a contrast here with how people view the loss of 'h' in words like *hill*, where the social statuses are the other way round. Pronouncing *h* is clearly a sign of higher social status than omitting it. This tells us very plainly that linguistic changes will be socially evaluated very differently depending on whether they stem from or are adopted by upper–class speakers or not. On the other hand, it is also apparent that television advertisers feel that pronunciations such as 'butterr' /bʌtər/ symbolize a wholesome, rural way of life and that they are therefore useful for the selling of certain supposedly wholesome foodstuffs, such as butter and bread.)

In the English-speaking world as a whole, of course, *r* is still pronounced before a consonant in most (but not all) parts of the USA, Canada, Ireland and Scotland, since the innovation has not yet reached these areas. It is *not*, however, pronounced before a consonant in Australia or (for the most part) New Zealand, since by the time the first immigrants from the south of England left for the southern hemisphere, the change had already taken place.

In this chapter, we use the presence or absence of 'r' in words like *arm* as a way of delineating the Central Lancashire area, in the North, and the Southwest areas, in the South (see below for definitions of these areas).

Some interesting consequences have flowed from this loss of 'r' in Modern Dialects. One of the most interesting is the development of what is sometimes called the 'intrusive 'r'. What happened was this. The change which originally took place in the London and East Anglian dialects was that 'r' was dropped before a consonant or pause, but retained before a vowel. This meant that, while 'r' was lost altogether in words like *arm* and *tart*, words such as *tar* and *car* acquired two different pronunciations. If the *r* at the end of words like this came before a vowel in the next word, as in *Your car is very good*, then the 'r' at the end of *car* was pronounced. But if it occurred before a pause, as in *You've got a good car*, or before a consonant, as in *Your car looks very good*, then the *r* was not pronounced. We thus had alternation between 'carr' /kaːr/ and 'cah' /kaː/.

As it happens, this alternation occurred at the end of words which ended in one of only a small number of vowels: it was found, as we have seen, in words such as *car* which contain the 'ah' vowel /aː/; it was also found, for example, in words like *four* and *more* with the 'aw'

56

vowel /ɔː/; words like *near* and *fear*, which have the 'ee-a' vowel /ɪə/; and words like *better* and *ladder*, which end in the 'uh' vowel /ə/. Thus:

r pronounced	r not pronounced
car engine	car port
four o'clock	four thirty
near it	near them
better off	better liked

Subsequently, a very interesting development took place which had the effect of regularizing the language. By analogy with words that had formerly had 'r' in their pronunciation (and which still had *r* in the spelling), words which did not have 'r' but which ended in one of these same four vowels came to be treated in the same way. (This sort of regularization is a common process in language change.) That is, words like *Shah* and *bra*, *law* and *saw*, *idea* and *Korea*, *Canada* and *Angela*, came to have two pronunciations also, to bring them into line with *car*, *four*, *near* and *better*. Speakers therefore now say 'That's a good idea' but 'The idear is good'. Thus:

r pronounced	r not pronounced
bra-r advert	bra strap
saw-r it	saw them
idea-r of	idea for
Angela-r Evans	Angela Smith

The 'r', moreover, may also appear in the middle of a word if the next syllable begins with a vowel: compare 'soar' – 'soaring' with 'draw' – 'drawring'.

In the case of words like *near* which have an r in the spelling, the 'r' which appears if the next word begins with a vowel is known as a **linking** 'r' while the 'r' that appears in words like idea is known as an **intrusive** 'r'. In fact they are actually one and the same phenomenon. It is simply the case that those modern accents of English which have lost the 'r' in *cart* – we can call them 'r-less accents' – have a process which automatically inserts an 'r' between two words if the first word ends in 'ah' /aː/, 'aw' /ɔː/, 'ee-a' /ɪə/ or 'uh' /ə/, and the second word begins with a vowel. Because this is a highly automatic process, it is one which most speakers are not aware of, unless they have their attention drawn to it. But of course it is a process which occurs only in the r-less accents. R-ful accents (as they are sometimes called), in places like the southwest, USA and Scotland, do not have this feature, because they have not undergone the loss of 'r' which started the whole process off in the first place. Speakers of r-ful accents therefore often comment on the intrusive-'r' phenomenon as a peculiar aspect of the accents of England. One can, for example, hear Scots ask 'Why do English people say "Canadarr"?'. English people of course do not say 'Canadarr', but those of them who have r-less accents do mostly say 'Canadarr and England' /kænədər ən ɪŋglənd/.

THE PRONUNCIATION OF *NG* IN *SINGER*

In most dialects of English around the world, the *g* in words like *long*, *bang*, *sing*, etc., is no longer pronounced e.g. [lɒŋ]. In these dialects *singer* and *finger* do not rhyme. There is a relatively large area of England, however, where the *g* is still pronounced – where, that is, a hard 'g' as in *get* can be heard at the end of words like *long* [lɒŋg]. In this area, words like *singer* and *winger* do rhyme with *finger*.

This is the original English pronunciation, which is reflected in the spelling which we still use, but which has been lost in pronunciation in other forms of English for several centuries. Places where the 'g' is still retained include Liverpool, Manchester and Birmingham. Birmingham is therefore actually called 'Birming-g'm' [bœːmɪŋgəm] by its inhabitants. This feature operates as a defining characteristic of the Central Lancashire, Merseyside, Northwest Midlands and West Midlands dialect areas (see map 13).

THE PRONUNCIATION OF *EW* IN *FEW*

Most people in England these days pronounce the word *super* as 'sooper' /suːpə/, but they are probably aware that there is an alternative pronunciation 'syooper' /sjuːpə/ which is still used by some speakers. This alternation is the result of a historical process whereby the 'y' sound /j/ has gradually been lost over the centuries before the long 'oo' vowel in certain groups of words. At an earlier stage in the language's history, for example, words like *rude* and *rule* were pronounced 'ryood' /rjuːd/ and 'ryool' /rjuːl/, but in modern English the 'y' sound has been lost before 'oo' where it occurs after *r*, and the same

Map 13   Areas where the pronunciation 'ngg' occurs in *singer*

is mostly true of words like *lute*, where the 'y' used to occur after *l*. Also, as we have seen, the loss is now spreading in England to words containing 'syoo', so that there is some vacillation about the pronunciation of words like *super*, *suit*, *sue*. In the English of London, moreover, this 'y' sound has also been lost after n, giving *news* pronounced as 'noos' /nuːz/, and in many forms of American and Canadian English it has also been lost after *t* and *d*, giving *tune* as 'toon' /tuːn/ and *duke* as 'dook' /duːk/.

Map 14   Areas where *few* is pronounced as 'foo'

However, there is one area of England where this change has spread further and affects this sound after *all* consonants in the language. In this area, not only is *news* 'noos' and *tune* 'toon', but *few* is 'foo' /fuː/, *pew* 'poo' /puː/, *beauty* 'booty' /buːtiː/, *view* 'voo' /vuː/, *music* 'moosic' /muːsɪk/, *huge* 'hooge' /huːdʒ/ and *cue* 'coo' /kuː/. This pronunciation has become well known in recent years through the television advertising of supposedly 'bootiful' poultry from the area in

Map 15   *Coffee*. 'i' in some northern areas vs 'ee' elsewhere

question, which covers Norfolk and parts of Suffolk, Essex, Cambridgeshire, Northamptonshire, Bedfordshire, Leicestershire, Lincolnshire and Nottinghamshire, and includes the towns of Norwich,
Cambridge and Peterborough (see map 14). It is used here as a defining
characteristic of our dialect regions of East Midlands, South Midlands
and East Anglia.

THE PRONUNCIATION OF *EE* IN *COFFEE*

The Central North, Central Lancashire, Northwest Midlands and Central Midlands areas are distinguished from all the other accent areas by their pronunciation of the final syllable in words such as *coffee*, *city*, *seedy*, *money* (see map 15). In most parts of the country the vowel in this syllable is 'ee' /iː/, so that in a word like *seedy* we have the same vowel in each syllable: 'seedee' /siːdiː/. In these four central northern regions, however, the vowel that is found in this final syllable is the short 'i' vowel /ɪ/ (or perhaps some other short vowel such as 'e' /e/) so that it is in words like *city* that the same vowel occurs in both syllables: 'citti' /sɪtɪ/. In this respect, these four northern areas again appear to have retained the original English pronunciation, which is still also found in the non-regional BBC and upper-class accents. It is interesting to note that the northern areas which have the newer 'ee' pronunciation are all in areas around coastal cities – Liverpool, Hull and Newcastle.

THE PRONUNCIATION OF *A* IN *GATE*

The long 'a' vowel /eɪ/ in words such as *gate* and *face* used to be a monophthong [ɛ:] in all varieties of English. This monophthong or pure vowel, however, has in the last 200 years or so begun to change into a diphthong of the type 'eh-ee' [eɪ] or 'a-ee' [æɪ]. This process started in the southeast of England, and it is in the London region where it has become most marked, with very broad diphthongs resembling 'ah-ee' [aɪ]. From there it has spread outwards until today we can say that most southern and midland areas have diphthongs of varying degrees of broadness (see map 16). The other regions furthest away from London – in the North and far Southwest – have not yet been influenced by this development and still for the most part retain monophthongs. A typical Lancashire pronunciation of *gate*, for instance, can be represented as 'gairt' or 'geht' [gɛ:t]. We employ this pronunciation feature to distinguish between the far Northern subregions of the North of England, on the one hand, and the Central sub-regions, on the other.

Map 16 *Gate*

THE PRONUNCIATION OF *L* IN *MILK*

The final feature that we employ in distinguishing between different Modern Dialects of English in England has to do with the pronunciation of *l* where it occurs after a vowel in words like *milk*, *hill*, *roll*, *ball*, etc. In a large area of southeastern England (see map 17), this consonant has acquired a short '00'-like vowel in front of it, or, especially in London itself, has disappeared altogether, leaving only the '00' behind:

milk	'mi-o͞olk' [mɪʊɫk] or 'mi-o͞ok' [mɪʊk]
hill	'i-o͞ol' [ɪʊɫ] or 'i-o͞o' [ɪʊ].

This is a relatively recent change, and one that is spreading quite rapidly. It has also had some interesting consequences for vowels generally. In the heart of this area – London itself – words ending in *-ill* and *-eel* such as *fill* and *feel* may now be pronounced identically: 'fi-o͞o(l)' [fɪʊ ~ fɪʊɫ]. And in all of this region there is a tendency for short

Map 17 *Milk*

'o' and long 'o' to become the same before an *l*:

doll 'do-ŏŏl' [dʌʊ]
dole 'do-ŏŏl' [dʌʊ]

Words such as *dull* may even acquire the same pronunciation, and there is also a tendency for words like *pull* and *Paul* to become the same. We are probably seeing here the beginnings of a whole new change in the

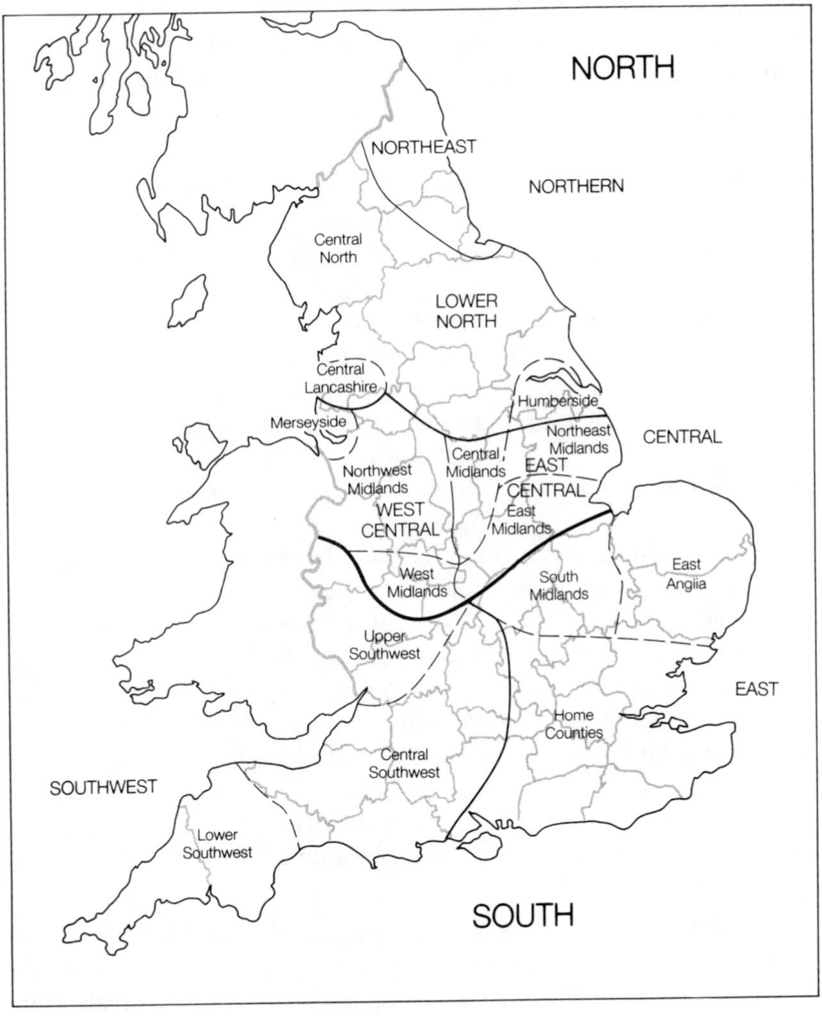

Map 18 Modern Dialect areas

language that will lead to the disappearance of '1' in these words altogether in the same way that 'r' began to disappear 200 years ago in words like *arm*.

The Overall Picture

If we now put together the above seven features and draw a composite accent map of England, we arrive at the pattern of accent differentiation shown in map 18, which gives us an illustration of the sixteen Modern Dialect regions of England. Note that few of them are identical with Traditional Dialect regions. These areas have the following names and contain the following towns and cities:

Northeast	Newcastle, Durham, Sunderland, Middlesbrough
Central North	Carlisle, Lancaster, Leeds, Bradford, York, Sheffield
Central Lancashire	Blackburn, Burnley, Accrington
Humberside	Hull, Scunthorpe, Grimsby
Merseyside	Liverpool, Birkenhead
Northwest Midlands	Derby, Stoke-on-Trent, Chester, Manchester
West Midlands	Birmingham, Wolverhampton, Walsall
Central Midlands	Nottingham, Leicester
Northeast Midlands	Lincoln, Louth
East Midlands	Grantham, Peterborough
Upper Southwest	Gloucester, Hereford
Central Southwest	Bristol, Salisbury
Lower Southwest	Plymouth, Exeter, Truro
South Midlands	Bedford, Northampton, Cambridge
East Anglia	Norwich, Ipswich
Home Counties	London, Brighton, Dover

The overall classification and grouping of Modern Dialects is given in figure 3.1. As we have seen, the major split is into dialects of the NORTH and SOUTH. The dialects of the SOUTH are further divided into those of the **Southwest**, which form a recognizable unity, and which are all characterized by the pronunciation 'arrm' /aːrm/ for *arm*, whereas those of the **East** have 'ahm' /aːm/.

The dialects of the NORTH are divided into the generally more conservative dialects which we label **Northern**, and those, mostly Midlands, dialects which we label **Central**, and which have the diphthong 'mayd' /meɪd/ in *made* rather than the older and more northerly form 'mehd' /meːd/. Within the Central dialects we distinguish between the **West Central** sub-group – the dialects of the Liverpool, Manchester, Derby and Birmingham areas, which all have the 'longg' /lɒŋg/ pronunciation for *long*; and the dialects of the **East Central** sub-group, associated with the areas of Nottingham, Leicester, Lincoln and Peterborough, which have 'long' /lɒŋ/ for *long*.

It must be remembered that the boundaries of the regions are in actual fact (not nearly so clear-cut) as they appear from the map. A number of places are actually rather hard to allocate to regions. Sheffield, for example, is in the Central North but has affinities with the East Midlands, Central Midlands and Northwest Midlands, while Cambridge could really fall in either East Anglia or South Midlands. Similarly, Reading and Bournemouth fall into the Home Counties if one considers younger speakers but into the Eastern Southwest if one

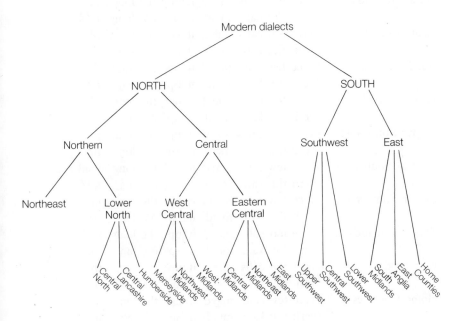

Figure 3.1

looks at older people, while Worcester is marginal as between West Midlands and Central Southwest – and so on.

To summarize the pronunciation characteristics of each of the regions, we give sixteen different regional versions of the sentence *Very few cars made it up the long hill*:

Table 3.1

Northeast	Veree few cahs mehd it oop the long hill
	/veriː fjuː kaːz meːd ɪt ʊp ðə lɒŋ hɪl/
Central North	Veri few cahs mehd it oop the long ill
	/verɪ fjuː kaːz meːd ɪt ʊp ðə lɒŋ ɪl/
Central Lancashire	Veri few carrs mehd it oop the long ill
	/verɪ fjuː kaːrz meːd ɪt ʊp ðə lɒŋ ɪl/
Humberside	Veree few cahs mehd it oop the long ill
	/veriː fjuː kaːz meːd ɪt ʊp ðə lɒŋ ɪl/
Merseyside	Veree few cahs mayd it oop the longg ill
	/veriː fjuː kaːz meɪd ɪt ʊp ðə lɒŋg ɪl/
NW Midlands	Veri few cahs mayd it oop the longg ill
	/verɪ fjuː kaːz meɪd ɪt ʊp ðə lɒŋg ɪl/
West Midlands	Veree few cahs mayd it oop the longg ill
	/veriː fjuː kaːz meɪd ɪt ʊp ðə lɒŋg ɪl/
Central Midlands	Veri few cahs mayd it oop the long ill
	/verɪ fjuː kaːz meɪd ɪt ʊp ðə lɒŋ ɪl/
NE Midlands	Veree few cahs mayd it oop the long ill
	/veriː fjuː kaːz meɪd ɪt ʊp ðə lɒŋ ɪl/
East Midlands	Veree foo cahs mayd it oop the long ill
	/veriː fuː kaːz meɪd ɪt ʊp ðə lɒŋ ɪl/
Upper Southwest	Veree few carrs mayd it up the long ill
	/veriː fjuː kaːrz meɪd ɪt ʌp ðə lɒŋ ɪl/
Central Southwest	Veree few carrs mayd it up the long iooll
	/veriː fjuː kaːrz meɪd ɪt ʌp ðə lɒŋ ɪʊl/
Lower Southwest	Veree few carrs mehd it up the long ill
	/veriː fjuː kaːrz meːd ɪt ʌp ðə lɒŋ ɪl/
South Midlands	Veree foo cahs mayd it up the long iooll
	/veriː fuː kaːz meɪd ɪt ʌp ðə lɒŋ ɪʊl/
East Anglia	Veree foo cahs mayd it up the long (h)ill
	/veriː fuː kaːz meɪd ɪt ʌp ðə lɒŋ (h)ɪl/
Home Counties	Veree few cahs mayd it up the long iooll
	/veriː fjuː kaːz meɪd ɪt ʌp ðə lɒŋ ɪʊl/

These are the criteria we employ in establishing our sixteen major regions, but of course the regions differ also in many other respects, and other features could have been employed. For example, as we saw in chapter 2, it is well known to people who live in England that there is a clear difference in the way in which words like *path, laugh, grass* and *dance* are pronounced in the north and south of England. In the north, they are pronounced with a short 'a' /æ/ – that is, with the same vowel as in *cat*. In the south, on the other hand, they are pronounced with a long 'ah' /aː/ – that is, with the same vowel as in *calm*. If we drew a line across England to demonstrate this contrast, it would leave the following regions in the Northern area: Northeast, Central North, Central Lancashire, Merseyside, Humberside, Northwest Midlands, Central Midlands, East Midlands and West Midlands. That is, this feature could be used to divide England into the two major regions of North and South in the same way as the vowel of *mud*, although the two features do not exactly coincide in the Midlands areas.

In the case of 'a' /æ/ versus 'ah' /aː/, however, there is a further complication. This is that, in actual fact, what we have just been saying about the south of England is something of a simplification. It is true that in East Anglia, South Midlands and the Home Counties, words like *path* have 'ah' /aː/ rather than the 'a' /æ/ of *cat*. We cannot really say this, however, of the Southwest regions. In much of these three regions, 'a' /æ/ and 'ah' /aː/ are not distinct vowels. That is, while both the North, on the one hand, and the Home Counties, South Midlands and East Anglia, on the other, have two different vowels, the one in *cat, bad, ran* and the other in *calm, rather, banana*, the Southwestern areas have only the one vowel. As a consequence, the true local accents in these areas do not make any distinction between *Pam* and *palm, Sam* and *psalm*, and rhyme words such as *lager* and *swagger*: 'lahger [lagəɹ], 'swahger' [swagəɹ].

We can now look at the regions that we have set up in a little more detail, summarizing our discussions above, and noting further details where appropriate.

The North

NORTHERN DIALECTS

The Northeast The Northeast area contains the urban centres of Newcastle, Sunderland, Middlesbrough and neighbouring areas. As anybody who has heard English from this area will know, the accent is very distinctive, and can be rather hard for people from, especially, the south of England to understand until they get used to it.

Some of the best-known characteristics of the modern Northeast pronunciation include the following. The accent, as we have seen, does not have the diphthongal pronunciations of the long 'a' vowel in *made*, *gate*, *face* that are more typical of the south of England, and the same is true of long 'o' as in *boat*, *road*, *load*. We have used the spelling *mehd* above to indicate this fact. In broad Tyneside especially, however, words such as these actually tend to be pronounced with a vowel of the type 'ee-a' in *made* [mɪed], *gate*, and 'oo-a' in *boat* [buət], *road*: 'meead a feeace', 'looad the booat'. The long 'o' vowel can also be pronounced with a vowel which may make *boat* sound rather like 'bert' to outsiders, [bŏːt]. The long 'i' vowel of *bite* [bɛit] moreover, sounds rather like the long 'a' vowel of *bait* to people from further south.

In Tyneside, too, words such as *bird*, *shirt*, *work* are pronounced with the same 'aw' vowel as in *north*, *for*, so that, for example, *shirt* and *short* are identical [ʃɔːt]. This is probably the result of the 'Northumbrian burr' 'r' (see p. 39), which has now died out in Modern Dialect, having influenced preceding vowels. (On Teesside, on the other hand, there is the same merger between the vowels of *hair* and *her* which is found in Liverpool (see below).) Typically, also, words that have *al* in the spelling are pronounced with a vowel of the type 'ah', so that *all* is 'ahl' /aːl/ and *walk* is 'wahk' /waːk/. This point is illustrated by the well-known 'Geordie' (Tyneside) joke concerning the non-Geordie doctor who asks his patient if he is able to *walk*, which his patient interprets as a query about *work* and replies 'Wawk! I cannot even wahk yet!'

The Lower North   The **Central North** region covers a large area of northern England stretching from Carlisle down to Sheffield and covering Cumbria, most of Yorkshire and parts of Lancashire. It differs from the Northeast by not having 'ee' in *very*, of our diagnostic features.

The Central North also contains a sub-area in which an interesting type of consonantal change takes place in certain conditions. What happens is that the voiced consonants 'b', 'd', 'g', 'v', 'z' and 'j' change to their voiceless counterparts 'p', 't', 'k', 'f', 's' and 'ch' if they occur immediately before any of these same voiceless consonants. The area involved includes most of western Yorkshire, and covers the towns of Halifax, Huddersfield and Bradford (which its inhabitants therefore

call 'Bratford'), but also extends beyond to Leeds and York. People
from this area will say:

    "'E wood goh' ('He would go')   'red book' 'bad writer'

    but

    "'E woot coom' ('He would come')   'ret pen' 'bat singer'

and so on.

The **Central Lancashire** area is mainly differentiated from its
neighbours by the retention of 'r' in words like *arm*. This conservative
feature, as we have noted, is clearly receding, however, and if it
disappears altogether Central Lancashire will differ from Northwest
Midlands only in lacking diphthongs in *made* etc. Indeed, diphthongal
pronunciations of *made* and *boat*, originally a south of England feature,
have also gradually spread northwards over the past 200 years or so,
and it is therefore very likely that Central Lancashire, too, will eventually acquire these pronunciations. For the time being, however, we
can say that the modern Central Lancashire accent is still characterized by the pronunciation of our diagnostic sentence as 'Veri few
carrs mehd it oop the longg ill' /verɪ fjuː kaːrz meːd ˈɪt ʊp ðə lɒŋg
ɪl/.

Other Central Lancashire features include the pronunciation of
words such as *book* and *cook* with the long vowel of *cool* /buːk/ rather
than with the short vowel of *pull* /bʊk/. This pronunciation can also
be found in many parts of the Central North and even in the East
Midlands. At one time, words spelt with *oo* had the long 'oo' vowel in
all parts of the country, but in the last several centuries many of these
have become shortened, with different sets of words being affected in
different parts of the country. In the West Midlands, for instance, *tooth*
is often pronounced with the short vowel /tʊ/, while in East Anglia,
roof /rʊf/ and *proof* are pronounced with the short vowel. Even in the
BBC accent, there is some alternation with words such as *room*. In
respect Central Lancashire is a conservative accent.

This area also has a pronunciation of long 'i' as in *by* which is
a monophthong of the type 'ah' [aː] or 'ah-eh' [aɛ], e.g. *night*
/naɛt/. It also has a distinctive, very front 'ü' vowel [yː] (se
words like *boot* [byːt].

Humberside, as we have noted, is essentially the region dominated by the urban areas of Hull and Grimsby, and is a typical north of England accent differing from Central Northern mainly in having the more modern pronunciation with 'ee' /iː/ at the end of words such as *very*. It still for the most part lacks diphthongs in *made* etc., however, thus remaining distinct from the East Midland dialects to the south. It is also characterized by a pronunciation of words like *ride, time, file* with a vowel very different from the one in *write, type, fife* e.g. *night time* = 'nite tahm' [naɪt taːm]; *bike ride* = 'bike rahd' [baɪk raːd]. Hull has some features in which it resembles Tyneside, in addition to the 'ee' in *coffee*, including the pronunciation of long 'o' as in *boat* [bəːt], which may sound rather like 'bert' with some speakers. And in some ways its speech resembles that of Liverpool, with a tendency not to distinguish the vowels of *wear* and *were* (see the following section).

Central Dialects

West Central Across the other side of England from Humberside we also find a port city with an accent rather more 'modern' than that of its hinterland – Liverpool. The accent of Liverpool, one of the very largest cities in England, and its surrounding **Merseyside** area, is well known to most British people, and very distinctive. The accent is essentially based on that of the surrounding areas and has many similarities with those of the Central Lancashire and Northwest Midlands areas, but it also has a number of more southern features and, interestingly, many from the English of Ireland, especially Dublin. This is of course not surprising when it is remembered that Liverpool received very considerable Irish immigration, particularly during the nineteenth century.

The Merseyside accent is distinguished from that of Central Lancashire by being r-less and by having diphthongs in **made** etc. It is distinguished from both Central Lancashire and Northwest Midlands by having 'ee' at the end of *very* etc. – like the Northeast, Merseyside is an 'ee'-pronouncing island surrounded by a sea of accents which do not (yet) have this feature.

Other Merseyside features include the fact that there is no contrast between pairs of words such as *fair* [fɛː] and *fir* [fɛː], *hair* and *her*. One of the Beatles' songs rhymes the word *her* with *aware*:

I've just seen a face
I can't forget the time or place
Where we met.
She's just the girl for me
And I want the world to see
We've met.
Had it been another day
I might have looked the other way
And I'd have never been aware
But as it is I'll dream of her
Tonight.

Another rhymes *her* with *there*:

Oh we danced through the night,
And we held each other tight,
And before too long I fell in love with her.
Now I'll never dance with another,
Since I saw her standing there.[1]

The Liverpool comedian Ken Dodd was famous, too, for his catchphrase 'Whaire's me shairt?' [wɛːz mi ʃɛːt].

Merseyside English often has 'd' rather than 'th' /ð/ at the beginning of words such as *there*. And the consonants 'p', 't' and 'k' are very heavily aspirated so that *matter* sounds almost like 'masser' and *lock* sounds rather like the Scots word *loch* [lɒkx ~ lɒx]. These two features Liverpool has in common with Dublin, and they may well have come from there originally. The Merseyside accent area is currently expanding, with many areas surrounding Liverpool having older speakers with Central Lancashire, Northwest Midlands or Welsh accents but younger speakers with Merseyside speech.

The **Northwest Midlands** contains the region around Manchester, and includes also Cheshire and parts of Shropshire and Derbyshire as well as Staffordshire and the Potteries. The Traditional Dialects of these places may be very different from one another, but recent changes have made the Modern Dialects quite similar, although of course, as always, locals will still have no difficulty in distinguishing between different sub-areas.

The modern accent of this area is distinguished from the East Midlands by the pronunciation of 'ngg' in *long* /lɒŋg/ etc., and by

73

retaining the 'y' in *few* /fjuː/; and from the West Midlands area, which borders it to the south, by not having the newer 'ee' /iː/ pronunciation in *very* etc. Within the region itself we can note variation in the pronunciation of the diphthongs in items like *made* and *coat*, with the diphthongs getting wider the further south you go. Thus Derby accents differ from Manchester accents by having 'bah-oot' [baʊt] rather than 'baw-oot' [bɔʊt]as the pronunciation of *boat*. Within the Northwest Midlands, too, the Potteries area around Stoke is rather distinctive, retaining some of the characteristics of the older Traditional Dialect (see p. 42).

The **West Midlands** area focuses on Birmingham and is the most southerly of all the northern areas. As a consequence, although it has the distinctively northern pronunciations of *up* as 'oop' /ʊp/ and *dance* as 'dannce' /dæns/, it also has many other features that are more southern than northern, such as 'ee' in *very* and broad diphthongs in *made* and *boat*. These diphthongs are broader than those in Derby and Manchester, but not as broad as those in London.

In the West Midlands, the short 'i' vowel in *pit* is rather like a short version of 'ee' [pit]; and distinctively diphthongal pronunciations of some other vowels, as in the south, are also found, such as the pronunciation of 'ee' itself as 'uh-ee' as in see 'suh-ee' [səɪ], while the long 'i' vowel of *by* sounds a little like 'oi' [bɒɪ]. The 'er' vowel of *her*, *fur* is also rather distinctive [fœː], being pronounced with rounded lips rather like the French vowel in *oeuf* = 'egg'. Within the West Midlands, the so-called 'Black Country' area around Dudley still has a rather distinctive speech.

Under the influence of Birmingham, this accent region is currently expanding and we must expect in the future to see a number of these pronunciation features spreading out into surrounding areas, perhaps especially the Central Southwest.

East Central The **Central Midlands** is a demographically important area which runs from northern Nottinghamshire down to Leicester. It is distinguished from areas to the north by having diphthongs in *gate* etc., from the Northwest Midlands area by having 'ng' rather than 'ngg' in *singer*, and from accents to the east and south by not having 'ee' in *coffee*. Indeed, speakers in this area may even have short 'e' at the end of words such as this: 'coffeh' [kɒfɛ]. The diagnostic sentence in this area has the form 'Veri few cahs mayd it oop the long ill' /verɪ fjuː kaːz meɪd ɪt ʊp ðə lɒŋ ɪl/.

74

In the Central Midlands we can also note the same sorts of differ-ences between the north and south that we saw in the Northwest Midlands. Both Nottingham and Leicester have diphthongs in *made* and *coat*, but these are wider in Leicester than in Nottingham. In Loughborough, which is between Leicester and Nottingham, the diph-thongs are also intermediate.

The **Northeast Midlands** is a relatively small and largely rural Central area that focuses on the city of Lincoln. It has southern features such as diphthongs, albeit close ones, in *gate* [geɪt] and *boat* [boʊt], and 'ee' /iː/ in *coffee*, but northern features such as 'oop' /ʊp/ rather then 'up' /ʌp/. It is distinguished from accents in the East Midlands area to the south by retaining the 'y' in *few* /fjuː/. The diagnostic sentence here is pronounced 'Veree few cahs mayd it oop the long ill' /veriː fjuː kaːz meɪd ɪt ʊp ðə lɒŋ ɪl/.

The **East Midlands** area covers parts of Nottinghamshire, Lincoln-shire, Leicester, Northamptonshire and Cambridgeshire, and it in-cludes towns such as Grantham and Peterborough. It is characterized by the pronunciation of the diagnostic sentence as 'Veri foo cahs mayd it oop the long ill' /verɪ fuː kaːz meɪd ɪt ʊp ðə lɒŋ ɪl/. It is thus distinguished from the south of England accents (South Midland and East Anglia) which border on it by retaining 'oop' /ʊp/ as the pro-nunciation of *up*. And it differs from its neighbouring regions to the north and west by, amongst other things, having lost the 'y' sound /j/ in words such as *few* and *beauty*. Again the East Midlands demon-strates broader diphthongs in the south of the area, e.g. in Peterbor-ough and Oakham, than in the north, e.g. in Grantham and Newark.

Within the East Midlands, Corby has an interesting form of English which is the result of heavy immigration from Scotland. Some young people who have lived all their lives in this area nevertheless have some Scots features in their speech.

Note that there is also an interesting area at the southwestern end of this region, where Northamptonshire borders on Oxfordshire, War-wickshire and Leicestershire. Here many dialect areas meet and a number of dialect feature boundaries come together. Within the space of a few miles, 'foo' /fuː/ changes to 'fyoo' /fjuː/, 'ahm' /aːm/ to 'arrm' /aːrm/, 'mi-oõlk' [mɪʊɫk] to 'milk' [mɪɫk] and 'oop' /ʊp/ to 'up' /ʌp/.

The South

The major subdivision of the southern dialects is into those of the Southwest, which are characterized by the retention of 'r' in *arm*, and those of the East, which have 'ahm' /aːm/.

THE SOUTHWEST DIALECTS

The **Upper Southwest** area, which is almost identical to the Northern Southwest Traditional Dialect area, covers Herefordshire together with Shropshire as far north as Shrewsbury, and much of Gloucestershire and Worcestershire. Using our accent criteria, we would also have to include in this area a number of adjacent areas of Wales, as well as the Gower peninsula and south Pembroke areas of Wales, where settlement from England in earlier centuries can still be detected in local speech.

The **Central Southwest** covers parts of Gloucestershire, Buckinghamshire, Oxfordshire, Berkshire and Hampshire, and all of Wiltshire, Avon and Somerset. It thus includes the major city of Bristol. South-coast cities such as Southampton, Portsmouth and Bournemouth formerly came into this area too, but are now being increasingly influenced by the speech of the Home Counties as are also the more easterly regions of Oxfordshire and Berkshire.

Bristol speech is famous for the presence in this accent of a phenomenon known as the 'Bristol l'. In the Bristol area, words such as *America, India, Diana, Gloria* are pronounced with a final 'l' – 'Americal', 'Indial', 'Dianal', 'Glorial' – with the result that it was once said that there was a family of three sisters there called 'Evil, Idle and Normal'. Certainly, words such as *area* and *aerial*, *rumba* and *rumble*, *idea* and *ideal* are pronounced the same. Nobody can be sure quite why this is, but it may be an example of what dialectologists call **hypercorrection**. This happens when speakers try to acquire a pronunciation which they perceive as having a higher status than their own, but overdo it. An example is when northerners trying to speak with a southern accent change not only 'oop' /ʊp/ to 'up' /ʌp/ and 'booter' /bʊtə/ to 'butter' /bʌtə/ but also 'hook' /hʊk/ to 'huck' */hʌk/ and 'good' /gʊd/ to 'gud' */gʌd/. It may be that 'l' at the ends of words disappeared at some stage in Bristol, as a natural sound change, and was then restored even where it did not belong by speakers trying to talk 'correctly'.

The **Lower Southwest**, as we have seen, is more or less identical with the two southwestern peninsula counties of Devon and Cornwall. It would be a mistake, however, as with our other regions, to assume that speech was uniform throughout this region. Devon, in particular, is rather different from Cornwall, and within Cornwall the east is rather different from the west, where the Cornish language itself was spoken until the seventeenth or eighteenth centuries (see chapter 2). In Devon, but mostly not in Cornwall, the long 'i' vowel of *by* etc. is pronounced almost like 'ah' [baː] The major feature distinguishing the Lower Southwest from the Central Southwest is the pronunciation of long 'a' as a monophthong: *made* 'mehd' [meːd]

THE EAST

The **South Midlands** covers most of Northamptonshire, Bedfordshire and Cambridgeshire, together with part of Buckinghamshire, and is an area which is in many ways intermediate between north and south, east and west. Even though we are now in the southern 'up' /ʌp/ rather than northern 'oop' /ʊp/ area, it is still the case that diphthongs in *made*, *boat* tend to be broader in the south, around Bedford, than in the north.

The South Midlands is also one area of the country where the glottal stop [ʔ] is very common as a pronunciation of 't'. This way of pronouncing 't' in words like *better*, *water*, *bet*, *what* is very well known to be a feature of Cockney or London English. But it is also very common indeed elsewhere, and there is at least a possibility that it began as an innovation in the eastern counties of England rather than in London itself. Apart from the South Midlands, the glottal stop is also especially common in East Anglia and the Home Counties, and it is least common in the West Midlands, the Northwest Midlands and Merseyside. Everywhere, however, it seems to be on the increase, and it is undoubtedly going to be a very prominent feature of the pronunciation of English in Britain in the future. (It is also widespread in Scotland.) This pronunciation is often characterized as 'leaving out your *ts*', but it is not in fact the case that the 't' is actually omitted. If it were omitted, this would make a word such as *fleeting* in these accents sound the same as *fleeing*, which it does not. Rather it sounds like 'flee'ing', with the apostrophe standing for the glottal stop pronunciation. Similarly, *better* is pronounced 'be'er' [bɛʔə] and *water* 'wa'er' [wɔːʔə], etc. The glottal stop is a perfectly normal consonant sound which is used in many of the world's languages, but because it is a fairly recent addition to the inventory of English sounds, and one which began life amongst lower-class speakers, it tends for the moment to have low prestige and to be resisted, for instance by some school-teachers and parents.

The particularly diagnostic features of the **East Anglia** area are lack of 'y' /j/ in *few*, which differentiates it from the Home Counties, and presence of 'h' in *hill*, which differentiates it from all other English regions except the Northeast, although today 'h' is rapidly being lost. Some words which elsewhere have the long 'o' vowel may have in East Anglia the short 'oo' vowel of *pull*, so that *coat* /kʊt/ rhymes with *put* /pʊt/, and *road* with *good* (see also p. 45). Also typical of East Anglia is the lack of distinction between the vowels of *here* and *there*, so that *peer* sounds like *pair* [pɛː], *here* like *hair* [hɛː], and *deer* like *dare* [dɛː]. People in Norfolk, for instance, have been known to drink 'bare' /bɛː/ (*beer*) on Yarmouth 'pare' /pɛː/ (*pier*).

Note, too, the rhymes involving *hear*, *air*, *clear* and *there* as used by the Norfolk dialect poet John Kett:

> Then there's the baads; they allus sing their best
> When I go paast the barn agen the wood.
> Ah, more'n once I'a stopped there jus' to hear
> Their lovely songs what fill the evenin' air.
> That don't corst naathin', and that dew yer good!
>
> There in't much swale na shelter 'long that rood,
> Bar near that row o' over-hangin' trees.
> The wind acrorst them fields, that wholly blow;
> Yew ketch it where them hedges bin cut low;
> That waake yer up in Winter, when that freeze!
>
> But come the Summer, tha's a different taale.
> The sun strike warm, an skies above 're clear,
> The wind blow sorft, a-rustlin' trew the grass,
> An I hear bees a-buzzin' as I pass -
> Why, evrawhere yew look, there's beauty there.[2]

Within East Anglia, the dialects of the Fens are rather distinctive and form a transition zone to the dialects of the South Midlands and East Midlands. The southern parts of the East Anglian region similarly have accents which resemble those of the Home Counties in a number of respects, so that the most distinctively East Anglian accents are to be found in northern and eastern Norfolk and northeast Suffolk.

The **Home Counties** area centres on the counties immediately around London, but includes also parts of Hampshire, Berkshire and Buckinghamshire, and is currently the centre of many innovations that are occurring in English pronunciation, such as changes in the pronunciation of l (see p. 63). Home Counties English is distinguished by having very wide diphthongs in *made, boat;* by a pronunciation of long 'i' as in *by* which is rather like 'oi' [ɒɪ]; and by a pronunciation of short 'u' in *up* which is rather like short 'a' [ap].

Another feature which is also spreading outwards from the Home Counties rather rapidly into the neighbouring regions is one which we have already noted in our discussion of Cockney in chapter 2, the loss of the distinction between the two 'th' sounds /θ, ð/ and 'f' and 'v'. Thus, *mother* is pronounced 'muvver' /mʌvə/ and *thing* is pronounced 'fing' /fɪŋ/. This was formerly confined to London speech, but now covers the whole of the Home Counties and is spreading so fast that younger speakers as far apart as Exeter, Manchester, Sheffield and Norwich have begun adopting this pronunciation since the 1980s.

Within the Home Counties, Londoners are still generally recognizable by, for example, their total loss of l in *hill* and *milk* 'mi-ook', but the Home Counties region is one which is clearly expanding at the present time, and we must expect in future years to see the influence of London speech, including the loss of 'l', spreading even further afield.

Trends

If we now compare the picture we have tried to draw in this chapter concerning Modern Dialects with the one we drew in chapter 2 for Traditional Dialects, we can see that a number of important things have been happening to English dialects in England. This becomes particularly clear if we compare map 9 (p. 34) with map 18 (p. 65). Here we can see that what was the most important British dialect boundary of all in the Traditional Dialects – the one that descended from Anglo-Saxon times and started on the east coast at the mouth of the Humber – seems to have disappeared completely.

This would appear at first sight to be a very dramatic development, but actually the boundary has not really disappeared. It has simply been displaced northwards to coincide today with, approximately, the English-Scottish border and with the original secondary *night*: 'neet' /niːt/ -'nicht' /nɪxt/ boundary (see p. 22). North of the national border you can still quite readily find speakers who say 'lang' for *long* and 'hame' for *home*. This is still therefore to be regarded as the most important dialect boundary in Britain. It is simply the case that it now divides Scotland from England rather than bisecting the north of England. It is probable that most British people would agree that the biggest dialect differences of all, and the most obvious, are today those that divide the English and the Scots.

As far as dialects in England are concerned, the original secondary Central-Southern boundary has now become the primary boundary. This is the line which divides those who say *past* as 'pahst' /paːst/ from those who say 'passt' /pæst/, and those who say *up* as 'up' /ʌp/ from those who say 'oop' /ʊp/. This line is a line which most English people are very well aware of and which they use informally to divide 'southerners' from 'northerners'. It *is* an important Modern Dialect boundary.

As for the smaller regions, we can see from comparing the two maps that the non-Traditional Dialect area of London has now expanded enormously to swallow up the old Southeast area, part of East Anglia, most of the Eastern Southwest, and most of the Central East, of which now only the South Midlands remain. This new London-based area we call the Home Counties Modern Dialect area.

Estuary English

It is this new Home Counties dialect area which has given rise to discussions in the British media during the past decade or so of a phenomenon journalists like to call 'Estuary English'. This is an inappropriate term which, however, has become widely accepted. It is inappropriate because it suggests that we are talking about a new variety, which we are not; and because it suggests that it is a variety of English confined to the banks of the Thames Estuary, which it is not. The label actually refers to the lower middle-class accents, as opposed to working-class accents, of the Home Counties Modern Dialect area. 'Estuary English' has obvious southeast of England features such as wide diphthongs in *made, boat*; the pronunciation of *l* in *milk* as 'mioolk' [mɪʊɫk] or [mɪʊk] (see p. 63), and the coming together of *doll* and *dole* etc.; and the glottal-stop pronunciation of *t* in *bet* [bɛʔ] and *what* [wɒʔ]. But it does not have features typical only of working-class accents, such as the glottal stop in in *better* and *water*, or the use of 'f' and 'v' in words like *mother* and *thing*. It has probably attracted so much journalistic attention since, because of the increasing democratization of British society, many people who in earlier generations would have abandoned their local accents for the BBC accent no longer do so. People who are upwardly socially mobile or who come into the public eye may still reduce the number of regional features in their speech, but they will no longer remove such features altogether. Many more people than was formerly the case can therefore now be heard in speaking in public situations, especially in the media, with lower middle-class regional accents. The most prominent of these accents are the lower middle-class accents of the southeast of England because this is the largest region of England in terms of population, and because there is a considerable metropolitan bias in the media, with most nationally available media being broadcast from London. There has also been a certain amount of upward social mobility in the last twenty years which has found people from lower middle-class backgrounds in socially prominent positions in which it would have been unusual to find them previously. As we have already seen, moreover, the Home Counties dialect area is much bigger than it used to be. It will continue to spread, I would guess, until it covers all of Hampshire, Bedfordshire, Cambridgeshire, Suffolk and parts of Northamptonshire.

This is part of a much bigger trend. What seems to have happened is that, parallel to the development of the large Home Counties dialect region centred on London whose lower middle-class accents have been referred to as 'Estuary English', we now have the development of similar areas elsewhere focussing on other urban centres. This pattern of the spreading out of urban dialect speech to form new dialect areas can be seen in map 18 particularly in the growth of the totally new dialect areas of the West Midlands (around Birmingham), Merseyside (around Liverpool) and Humberside. The Northwest Midlands area, too, is heavily influenced by Manchester, Stoke and Derby, while the Northeastern area has expanded to take in all the coastal urban areas from Newcastle down to Hartlepool, Stockton and Middlesbrough. Of course, there remain distinctive differences within all of these areas – no one from Middlesbrough would mistake a Tynesider for someone from Middlesbrough – but the accents are sufficiently similar to be grouped together, and sufficiently different from those of other areas. Londoners, for instance, might mistakenly think that Middlesbrough speakers were from Newcastle, but they would be much less likely to think that they were from, say, Sheffield.

The Future

As far as our different major dialect features are concerned, we can make the following predictions.

The 'ee' vowel in *very* is obviously spreading rather rapidly. Most Traditional Dialects in England, except in the far south, have (or had) short 'i' /ɪ/ in *very* (or even, in East Anglia, 'uh' /ə/, so that *very* 'verruh' /verə/ rhymed with *terror* /terə/). This has now been replaced in most of the South and Midlands by 'veree' /veriː/, which seems to be spreading northwards quite quickly. It has already, as we have seen, 'jumped' over intervening areas to the urban centres of Liverpool and Newcastle.

The pronunciation 'foo' /fuː/ for *few*, on the other hand, seems to be static geographically and is unlikely to spread. More likely, the 'foo' area will decline in size in the next decades.

We have also already seen that the pronunciation of *arm* as 'arrm' /aːrm/ is retreating into a smaller and smaller area every year, and our prediction has to be that 'r' is unlikely to survive in England in words of this sort for longer than a century or so.

The pronunciation of *made* as 'mayd' /meɪd/ rather than 'mehd' /meːd/, on the other hand, is becoming more widespread and seems destined to spread into Humberside, Central Lancashire and the Lower Southwest in the not too distant future. The pronunciation of *up* as 'up' /ʌp/ rather than 'oop' /ʊp/ may also be spreading northwards, though rather more slowly, while the 'longg' /lɒŋg/ pronunciation of *long* may be receding – but again rather slowly. What there is no doubt about, as we have already seen, is the very rapid spreading of the changes in the pronunciation of *l* in words such as *milk* to give 'mĭŏŏk'.

Of other features, we do not expect, on current evidence, the 'pahth' /paː/ pronunciation of *path* to spread much further, but the glottal stop pronunciation of *t*, as in 'be'er' [bɛʔə], *better*, seems certain to spread far and wide – it has quite recently arrived in Cardiff, for instance – as do the pronunciations 'bruvver' for *brother* and 'fing' for *thing*.

As for our dialect areas themselves, the growing importance of urban speech in the formation of Modern Dialects reflects changing demographic and economic patterns in England over the last 200 years, and we must expect this trend to continue. We can predict the survival of the Northeast area focussed on Newcastle, Merseyside focused on Liverpool, West Midlands focused on Birmingham, and Northwest Midlands focused on Manchester as distinctive areas. At the same time, we would expect the growth of a South Yorkshire region extending

Map 19   Possible future dialect areas

from the Pennines to Humberside; the disappearance of Central Lancashire as a dialect region; the contraction of the Lower Southwest and the Upper Southwest, and the growth of a new region focused on Bristol. East Anglia will probably also contract and the South Midlands disappear in the face of continuing expansion of the Home Counties area based on London.

A predicted possible scenario for the division of the major regional varieties of English English for the next century is given in map 19. Note that we can divide these possible future dialect areas into two groups: the seven major city-based regions of Newcastle, South Yorkshire, Manchester, Liverpool, East Midlands, Birmingham, and London; and the six more rural relic areas of North Lancashire and the Lake District, North Yorkshire, Lincolnshire, Norfolk, the Welsh Marches, and Cornwall and Devon.

Happily, however, it is certain that, whatever the exact form of future developments will be, there will never be total uniformity across the country, because innovations will always continue to spread and recede and thus continue to produce the rich mosaic of regional variation in pronunciation which has characterized England ever since English first became its language.

4

◆

The Grammar of English Dialects

4

In this chapter we concentrate particularly on the grammatical characteristics of the different Traditional Dialects, but we also discuss at
some length certain features of the grammar of the Modern Dialects.
As we saw in chapter 1, all dialects of English are grammatical. They
all have their individual rules of grammar and their grammatical
structures. The fascination for the student of English dialects lies in the
very wide degree of variation in these structures that can be found
between the dialects.

Grammatical Distinctions

Many dialects, for instance, have grammatical distinctions that are not
present in Standard English. The *this/that* demonstrative system of
Standard English, for example, is a two-way system which distinguishes only between things which are distant and things which are
near. It also distinguishes, of course, between singular and plural:

	singular	plural
near	this book	these books
distant	that book	those books

Many Nonstandard Modern Dialects employ *them* or *they* rather than
those:

them boys over there
they books on the table

The addition of *here* to the near forms and *there* to the distant forms is also common:

these here people
that there book

Interestingly, however, a number of Traditional Dialects differ from these systems in having a three-way distinction. For example, some northern dialects have:

	singular	plural
near	this	thir
far	that	tho
remote	yon/thon	yon/thon

while southwestern dialects may have systems such as:

	singular	plural
near	thease	theys
far	that	they
remote	thik	thik

This last form is illustrated in writing from Dorset:

When I awoke woone Mayday morn,
I vound an urge wi'in mee born,
To zee the beauteous countryzide
That's all round wer' I do bide.

Zoo I zet out wi' dog an' stick,
Mee 'ead wer' jist a trifle thick,
But good ole fresh air 'ad 'is zay
An' blowed thik trouble clean away.'[1]

On the other hand, many dialects do not observe certain grammatical differences that are present in Standard English. Very few dialects, for instance, distinguish between adverbs ending in *-ly*, such as *nicely*, and their corresponding adjectives. So, while Standard English has *she's a nice singer* but *she sings nicely*, most Nonstandard Dialects have *she's a nice singer* and *she sings nice*.

In some cases, Standard English differs from other dialects because it has lost older forms which have survived in some of the dialects, or because it has developed new forms, which have not (yet) penetrated into the dialects. Many dialects, for instance, still have forms such as *He's a-comin* rather than *He's coming*, where the *a-* is a very ancient survival from Anglo-Saxon times. And there are a number of Traditional Dialects which retain plural forms such as *housen* rather than the regular *houses* of Standard English.

Another example is provided by the way in which Standard English speakers say things like *I don't want any trouble* with only one negative (*n't*) while speakers of most other dialects use older forms such as *I don't want no trouble* with more than one negative. Standard English has similarly lost the capacity, amply illustrated in the works of Shakespeare in lines such as 'the most unkindest cut of all', to employ double comparatives and superlatives, while most Nonstandard Dialects continue to employ forms such as *He's more rougher than what you are* and *That's the most stupidest thing I've heard*.

In other cases, differences between Standard English and the Nonstandard Dialects are due to archaisms in Standard English which have been lost elsewhere, such as the retention of the ancient form *whom* (rather than *who* or some other form) as in *the woman whom I saw*. They may also be due to innovations in the Nonstandard Dialects which have not (yet) reached Standard English, such as the changing of irregular verbs to a regular pattern, as in *I drawed a picture* rather than *I drew a picture*. And of course the Nonstandard Dialects also differ from one another because of changes – the loss of old forms and the development of new ones – which have taken place in some of the dialects but not in others.

We now look in more detail at those aspects of the grammatical system of English which demonstrate differences of various types between the dialects.

Pronouns

PERSONAL PRONOUNS

We can begin to look at the pattern of differences between English dialects by examining first of all the personal pronouns – words such as *you, me, hers, our* and so on.

Table 4.1

	1	2	3	4	5
Singular	I	me	my	mine	myself
	you	you	your	yours	yourself
	he	him	his	his	himself
	she	her	her	hers	herself
	it	it	its	its	itself
Plural	we	us	our	ours	ourselves
	you	you	your	yours	yourselves
	they	them	their	theirs	themselves

The Standard English system of personal pronouns is as shown in table 4.1. Each pronoun has five different forms. The five forms of *I*, for example, could be used like this:

I want the book
Give it to *me*
It's *my* book
It really is *mine*
I want it for *myself*

Within the Modern Dialects, there are quite a few differences from this Standard English system which can be noted, some very widespread and some more geographically restricted.

One very widespread feature is the use of *me* rather than *my* in expressions such as *Where's me bike?* Indeed, this even occurs in Standard English, in colloquial styles, at least for some speakers. Another such feature is the use of *us* as a singular, which occurs colloquially as an indirect object, even in Standard English, in expressions such as *Give us a kiss* and *Lend us a fiver*, where *us* means *me*. In some Nonstandard Dialects, however, such as in the northeast, it is much more widely used than this as a singular pronoun, and sentences such as *He tapped us on the shoulder*, with *us* as the direct object, are quite normal.

Most of the Nonstandard Modern Dialects have also developed a system of reflexive pronouns – the *myself, yourself* series – which is different from that of Standard English. If you compare the pronouns in column 5 above with those in the other columns, you will see that the column 5 reflexive pronouns consist of the forms -self/-selves preceded by either form from column, as in *myself* or a form from column 2, as in *himself*. The Nonstandard Dialects have for the most part regularized this system by using only forms from column 3, the possessive pronouns. This give

singular	**plural**
myself	ourselves
yourself	yourselves
hisself	
heirselves	
herself	
itself	

in which *hisself* and *theirselves* are forms not found in Standard English.

Of Modern Dialect features which are less widespread, we can mention the use of *us* rather than *our* in parts of the north of England: *That's us bus over there*. And we can note the use in East Anglia and in the South Midlands of *that* rather than *it*, except where *it* occurs unstressed after verbs. Thus these speakers say:

I don't like it when that's raining

and

I don't want it – that's no good

This is also found in Eastern Counties Traditional Dialect as is illustrated in the writing from northeast Essex of the author of the *Essex Ballads*, Charles Benham:

There's olluz summat. When tha's wet
The corn git läid, the häy git sp'iled
And when tha's dry the lan' git set.
That fare to make me wholly riled.

You want it wet, tha's olluz fine,
You want it cowd, tha's olluz mild,
You want it dry, there's nought but räin,
That fare to make me wholly riled.[2]

Hisn and hern

If we now turn to forms that are more typical of Traditional Dialects, we can focus first on the possessive forms that are shown in column 4 on page 88: *mine, yours, hers,* etc. It will be seen that in Standard English all these forms end in -*s* except *mine.* In a large area of southern England, including Traditional Dialects from both the Western and Eastern branches, this system has been entirely regularized to follow the pattern set by *mine.* That is, all the forms end in -*n.* We thus have the system:

singular	plural
That's *mine*	That's *ourn*
That's *hisn*	That's *yourn*
That's *hern*	That's *theirn*

The Traditional Dialect areas from the Western branch which have this system are: the Wiltshire and Hampshire region of the Western Southwest, the whole of the Northern Southwest and Eastern Southwest areas, and the Berkshire and Sussex areas of the Southeast area. From the Eastern branch, it is the Northampton and Cambridgeshire area of the Central East which has this pattern. The Leicestershire area also has this feature. This area of the south of England is shown in map 20. Note that geographically peripheral areas of the south – Devon, Cornwall, East Anglia – do not have *hern, hisn, ourn, yourn, theirn,* which indicates that this was probably an innovation that started life somewhere in the centre of the country.

Thee and thou

Most languages of the world make a distinction between singular *you,* referring to one person, and plural *you,* referring to more than one. French, for example, has singular *tu* and plural *vous.* Norwegian has singular *du* and plural *dere* – and so on. All varieties of English at one time used to have this distinction too. *Thou* and *thee* were used for the singular, and *ye* and *you* were used for the plural. In the last 300 years or so, however, Standard English and the other Mainstream Dialects have lost this distinction, with *you* being extended to singular usage and *thou/thee* dying out.

Map 20   Areas where the possessive form ends in -*n*

The reason for this loss of *thou* has to do with a practice which is also common in languages around the world – the use of plural *you* to refer respectfully or politely to individual persons. Thus, although in French *tu* is singular and *vous* plural, it is normal to call individuals *vous* unless you know them well. In Standard English, this polite usage was so extensively practised that the original singular form was lost altogether,

91

and it is now no longer possible to distinguish grammatically between 'one' and 'more than one' *you.*

Some dialects, however, have repaired this loss. The Traditional Dialects of the Eastern Counties, for instance, have singular *you* but plural *you together* as in *Are you comin' together?* (with emphasis on *coming*) meaning *Are you* (plural) *coming?*

A number of dialects influenced by Irish English, such as the dialect of Liverpool, have similarly developed *youse* as a plural form of *you.* In true Merseyside dialect, as in Belfast and Dublin, *How are you?* can refer only to one person. If you want to know how a group of people are getting on, you have to ask *How are youse?*

Other Traditional Dialects, on the other hand, have never gone the way of Standard English as far as these pronouns are concerned, and have preserved the old distinction between *thou* and *you,* with *thou* being used to address an individual person one is familiar with. There are two major Traditional Dialect areas of England which have preserved this distinction – one northern area and one western area – although even here most Modern Dialects have lost or are losing it. The northern area consists of the Lower North (Cumbria, Durham, North Yorkshire and East Yorkshire) plus the Lancashire and Staffordshire areas, including the Potteries of the Central region. Parts of the South Yorkshire area have also kept the *thou* forms. The western area consists of the Northern Southwest, and the Western Southwest (Cornwall, Devon, Somerset, Dorset, Wiltshire, Hampshire), including the city of Bristol. Although these areas actually form a single contiguous zone (see map 21), we distinguish between them because the northern area has *thou* more commonly than *thee* as the singular pronoun, while the western area mostly has *thee* rather than *thou.* As map 21 shows, it is only in the south and east of England that Traditional Dialects have totally replaced *thou/thee* by *you,* while in Northumberland the usual Traditional Dialect form of the pronoun (singular and plural) is *ye.*

Traditional Dialects which preserve *thou/thee* normally also have distinctive verb forms of the type familiar from the King James version of the Bible, such as *thou hast, thou dost.* Traditional working-class Bristol dialect, for instance, has *cassn't?* = 'can't you?' from *canst thee not?*, and *dissn't?* = 'didn't you?' from *didst thee not?*. The Potteries area of northern Staffordshire has *ast?* = 'have you?' from *hast thou?*, and *thee coost* = 'you could' from *couldest.* The use of this singular pronoun is illustrated in the work of the northern dialect poet Samuel Laycock, who was born in Yorkshire and lived in Cheshire and Lancashire. Note

Map 21   *You* (singular)

that *thou* is spelt *tha*, and that the object and possessive forms of the
pronoun are *thee* and *thi* = 'thy', respectively:

> Thi feyther's noan been wed so long,
> An' yet tha sees he's middlin' throng
> Wi' yo' o.
> Besides thi little brother Ted,

We've one upsteers, asleep i' bed,
Wi' eawr Joe.

But tho' we've childer two or three,
We'll mak' a bit o' reawm for thee,
Bless thee, lad!
Th'art prattiest brid we have i' th' nest
So hutch up closer to mi breast:
Aw'm thi dad.[3]

The following is a folk-song in a version from western Derbyshire. Note the forms *asta?* = 'have you?', *dusta?* = 'do you?', *cossna* = 'can't'. The form *oh* means 'she' – see p. 101.

Asta seen aar Mary's bonnet?
It's a stunner, an' no mistak;
It's got red rooses raight on top,
An' tow big ribbons raight dairn t'back.

Dusta know, aar Mary, oh went ter choch on Sundee
An' the praycher
Eh prayched an' prayched an' prayched
Abairt aar Mary's bonnet.

An' aar Mary, oh stood up in choch an' sed:
'Ey up thae! It's bett'n'en thine
Thaa bawd-yedded tonnip -
Tha cossna get n'rooses rairnd thy bonnet!'[4]

For the pronunciations 'thae' = *thee*, *praycher* = *preacher*, 'raight' = right etc. see pp. 41–2.

PRONOUN GENDER IN THE SOUTHWEST

In Standard English, in other Mainstream Dialects, and in most Traditional Dialects, the same gender system operates: *he*, *him* and *his* refer to male persons and animals; *she*, *her* and *hers* refer to female persons and animals; and *it* and *its* refer to things. (There are a few exceptions, of course, such as *she* being used for ships.) However, in the southwestern dialect area of England – Eastern Southwest, Northern Southwest and Western Southwest – a rather different system operates in the Traditional Dialects. The striking thing to outsiders is the way in which things can be referred to as *he*. The way it works is that **count nouns** – individual things which can be picked up, moved around and counted – can be referred to as *he*:

He's a good hammer

while **mass nouns** – things which cannot be counted, such as *bread*, *butter*, *milk*, etc. (you don't normally say 'two breads') – are referred to as *it*:

Pass the loaf – he's over there

but

I likes this bread – it's very tasty

We can see this illustrated in some dialect poetry.

Zo I 'ad me 'air done, Lor' what a game!
I thought me 'ead were on vire.
But 'twas worth it, mind, I looked quite zmart –
I even got a glance vrom the Squire.

I got out me best dress, but he were tight,
Zo I bought meself a corset.
Lor', I never thought I'd breathe agin,
But I looked zo zlim 'twas worth it.[5]

Here *he* refers to the dress.

PRONOUN EXCHANGE

Another feature of southwestern dialects is sometimes known as pronoun exchange. This is a feature, however, which is also shared by the Traditional Dialect of Essex, suggesting perhaps (see map 22) that it was once more widespread than it is today in the southern areas of England. In these dialects, the pronouns *he, she, we, they* can occur as objects as well as subjects of verbs. That is, one can say:

95

Map 22   Pronoun exchange (PE) areas

John saw they
Bill gave it to she

and so on. Similarly, the pronouns *him*, *her*, *us* can occur, unlike in other dialects, as subjects of verbs:

Us be a-goin
Her don't like it

This is shown in some verses from the same poem from Dorset by Devina Symes:

> Well, we staggered whome at 'alf-past dree,
> A-zinging all the way.
> Me 'usband gi' I a kiss,
> The vust since me widding-day.
>
> Zo I be lookin' varward to next year,
> To the partee an' all its vun.
> I'd like to thank the Squire ver his kindness,
> An' wish a Merry Christmas to he, an' everyone.[6]

In some of these dialects the rule is that the Standard English subject pronouns occur when the pronoun is emphasized, while the 'object' forms occur as subjects when the pronoun is not emphasized:

> Give it to *he*, not *they*

It may, however, be more complicated than that. For example, in parts of Somerset we find sentences like:

She give it to 'er, didn' 'er?
and *'Er give it to 'er, didn' 'er?*   'She gave it to her, didn't she?'

but *'E give it to un, didn' a?*
and *'E give it to 'e, didn' a?*   'He gave it to him, didn't he?'

In South Devon the Traditional Dialect system is currently as shown in table 4.2. This is complicated by the fact that, actually, *ee* (= 'you'), from *ye/thee* is pronounced identically with *he* = 'e'. Note that in most of these dialects, unstressed *he/him* is *un*, which goes back to Old English *hine* = 'him rather than Old English *him*, as in Standard English, which originally meant 'to him'.

We thus find usages such as:

> Her'll do it
> You'll come, will ee?
> I seed 'n

97

Table 4.2

		Subject		Object	
		Unstressed	*Stressed*	*Unstressed*	*Stressed*
Singular	1	I	I	me	me
	2	ee	you	ee	ee
	3m	he	he	un	he
	3f	her	her	her	her
	3n	t'	it		
Plural	1	us	us	us	us
	2	ee	you	ee	you
	3	they	they	'em	they

> I never seed he, I seed they
> Us'll go
> I seed 'em
> It's good, so t'is

In South Devon, also, count nouns such as *hammer* are referred to as *he/'n*. The possessive pronouns are also interesting. They are of the form:

	singular	**plural**
1	me	our
2	yer	yer
3m	he's	their
3f	her	
3n	its	

So Standard English *his book* is *he's book* (or rather *e's book*) However, where the pronoun *he* refers to a non-human unit or count noun, then the possessive is not *he's* but *of un*. Thus:

> referring to John: *he's book*
> referring to the hammer: *the handle of un*

As we saw above, this 'pronoun exchange' system where usage depends on emphasis is also found across the other side of London from the Eastern Southwest area in the Traditional Dialect area of Essex. This suggests that the system might have been more widespread formerly, before the spreading out from London of forms closer to Standard English. The following verses from the *Essex Ballads* written in the 1890s in the dialects of the rural areas around Colchester show this system very clearly:

Jealous? What me? O' sech as *har* indeed!
Nao, that I know I ent, so there. Good lor',
Upon my life I think I never seed
A gal look sech a bag o' rags afore.

Tha's where they're gooin', are they? Pas' the mill,
Along the fiel' path leadin' tard the woods:
I'll give *he* what for some däy, that I will,
For walkin' out 'ith that ere bit of goods.

J'yer hear *him* call 'Good arternune' to me?
He think he's doin' of it there some tune.
Next time I ketch *him* out along o' *she*,
Blest if I don't give *he* 'good arternune'.[7]

And:

A rum un? I sh'd rather think he were!
T'd taike yer all yer time to tackle *he*.
An' langwidge? Lor', j'yer ever hear *him* swear?
A mark on swearin'? Ah, sir, that he be.

You on'y got to säy 'I bet yer don't',
An' Bill'll do it, don' care what it be.
He'll best yer, too, I'm bothered if he 'ont;
There's no man livin' dussent tackle *he*.[8]

And:

One of 'em come to Master at the Hall,
An' arst all manner stuff, and writ it down.
A great owd book he'd got, to howd it all,
An' take it up to *thäy* in Lunnon town.

99

Cummish'ner, I'd cummish'ner *him*, I would,
I could a made *he* look, I could to-däy.
What do he knaow? He carn't do *we* nao good,
Tellyerferwy – acos he carn't, tha's why.[9]

In the work of Cornish dialect poet Bernard Moore we can read:

Ruth Pemwarne be a brave rich woman
Her lives in a cottage with a warpely door;
Her've got four childer, not counten the baby,
An' there bain't no tellin' but *her* might have more.

Miss Tregear have a room for dinin'
An' a room for drawin' where *her* doesn' draw
An' a room where books be shut in cupboards
An' other *us* don't know what they'm for.[10]

A very recent example is:

When I were young if I felt sad
or troubled in the mind
I did use to suck a grass
and in it comfort find.

Now we sprays with chemicals
and it do seem to *I*
That he who sucks a grass today
is very like to die.[11]

OTHER TRADITIONAL DIALECT PRONOUN FORMS

We have already seen that most Modern Dialects have reflexive pronouns of the type *hisself, theirselves*. In the Eastern Central Traditional Dialect area, however, and to a certain extent also in the corresponding Modern Dialects, forms with *-sen/-sens* rather than *-self/selves* are found. Here is an example from the Lincolnshire region:

Cum in, lass, A'm real pleased to see ye,
    yah're welcome as flowers i' Maäy.
Cum an' sit *yersen* down o' the soäfy –
    not that end – a bit tother waäy;

100

The cushions is clean an' A doän't want'm ruckled,
   thaäy're fresh weshed ya see.
A doan't oftens git many callers,
   soä A'm glad that yah've comed to see me.[12]

In the Lancashire area, and to a certain extent in the neighbouring Staffordshire area, the word *hoo* is found instead of *she*. *Hoo* comes from the Old English word for 'she', *hēo*:

When I put little Sally to bed,
Hoo cried, 'cose her feyther weren't theer,
So aw kiss'd little thing, an' aw said
Thae'd bring her a ribbin fro' th' fair.'[13]

Finally, it may still be possible, in the area on the border between Somerset and Dorset, to find Traditional Dialect speakers who say *itch* or *utch* rather than *I*. Certainly, there were such speakers in the 1950s. *Utch* is a very interesting form which goes back to the original Old English word for 'I', which was *ik* or *ic*, later *ich* (pronounced 'itch'). (Compare Dutch *ik*, German *ich*.) In most English dialects, including Standard English, *ik/ich* became *i*, now spelt *I*, but in the southwest the -*tch* remained. In these dialects – as can be noted in Shakespeare's representations of rustic speech – forms such as *cham* = 'I am', *chill* = 'I will', *chall* = 'I shall' were usual.

Verbs

Present-tense verbs in Standard English are peculiar in that they take the ending -*s* in the third-person singular- after *he*, *she* or *it*, for instance – but nowhere else. Thus we have:

I take	but	*he takes*
you take		
we take		
they take		

In many of the dialects, this irregularity is not found. In the East Anglian area, for example, including in Modern Dialects, present-tense verbs are entirely regular and have no -*s*, ending at all:

He like her
She want some
That rain a lot there

This was formerly also true of the Traditional Dialects of the Essex area, as can be seen from the *Essex Ballads* on pp. 99–100.

In very many western and northern dialects, on the other hand, in Traditional Dialects and Modern Dialects alike, the regularization is the other way, with all persons of the present-tense verb taking -*s*:

I wants it
We likes it
They sees them

Some dialects tend not to have -s when the subject of the verb is a noun – *The boys see them every day* – but do have it when it is a pronoun – *They sees them every day.*

Traditional Dialects also retain a number of other interesting forms. For example, it is well known that Standard English used to have -*eth* as the third-person singular ending, rather than -*s* (which was originally a northern dialect form), until the 1600s. This form, familiar from Shakespeare and the Bible, has of course now disappeared from modern Standard English, but it can still be found in some Traditional Dialects. The *Survey of English Dialects*, for example, working in the 1950s and 1960s, found verbs such as *weareth* = 'wears' and *dooth* = 'does' in Devon and Cornwall. It is also possible to find Traditional Dialects in which older plural verb forms in -*en* are retained, as in *we putten, they cutten* = 'we put, they cut'. These are particularly common in the Staffordshire dialect area.

Another interesting Traditional Dialect feature comes from the southwest of England, and in particular the Somerset and Dorset sub-region of the Western Southwest. In these dialects, present tense verb forms are of two types:

I sees and *I do see*

The same is also true of past-tense forms:

I seen and *I did see*

The point is that there is a difference of meaning between these alternative forms, as illustrated in the following sentences:

> I sees the dentist tomorrow
> I seen the dentist last week

versus

> I do see the doctor every day
> I did see the doctor every day

The simple verb forms – *sees, seen* – refer to single events or actions. The other forms – *do see, did see* – refer to actions or events that are repeated or habitual. (Note that *I do see* etc., is pronounced with emphasis on *see*, that is 'I da **see** him'.) These Traditional Dialects, then, have a grammatical distinction which is not available as such in other dialects, including Standard English.

The southwestern dialects also have another very interesting feature to do with the verb, this time found in Devon and Cornwall as well as Somerset and Dorset. In these dialects, infinitives such as *to go, to see, to sew* take a *-y* ending if they have no object. Thus, in Dorset dialect, one can say:

> *Can you zew up thease zeam?* = 'Can you sew up this seam?'

but

> *Can you zewy?* = 'Can you sew?'

The famous Dorset dialect poet William Barnes writes

> *The cat vell zick an' woulden mousy* =
> 'The cat fell sick and wouldn't mouse'

Similarly, in Devon we find:

> *There idden many can sheary now* =
> 'There aren't many who can shear now'

Dialects of the Northumberland area, on the other hand, have interesting structures such as:

I divent knao – I might could do it =
'I don't know – I might be able to do it'

He wouldn't could've worked, even if you had asked him =
'He wouldn't have been able to work, even if you had asked him'

The girls usually make me some, but they mustn't could have made   any today =
'The girls usually make me some, but they can't have been able   to make any today'

These combinations of *might* and *could*, *must* and *could*, and so on, are also found in Scotland and in a number of areas of the USA, including Texas.

NEGATIVE VERB FORMS

The Nonstandard Modern Dialects have a number of ways of making verbs negative which are not found in Standard English. The most famous of these is *ain't*, which is also found in the Traditional Dialects. In many dialects, forms with pronunciations such as 'ain't', 'en't', 'in't' occur, and have two different functions. One is to act as the negative form of the present tense of *be*:

Standard English	Nonstandard Dialects
I'm not coming	I *ain't* coming
You *aren't* coming	You *ain't* coming
He *isn't* coming	He *ain't* coming

The other function is to act as the negative present tense of the auxiliary verb *have* which is used to form perfect-tense verbs such as *I have done it*. Thus:

Standard English	Nonstandard English
I *haven't* done it	I *ain't* done it
You *haven't* done it	You *ain't* done it
He *hasn't* done it	He *ain't* done it

104

Note that this does not apply to the full verb *have*. The negative of *I have my breakfast at 8* is *I don't have my breakfast at 8* and not **I ain't my breakfast at 8*. There is some controversy about the origins of *ain't*, but it is an old verb form which used to have more social status than it does now, and which probably is a form of *aren't* and/or *amn't* and/ or *haven't*.

The form *aren't* itself also has one usage in some of the Nonstandard Dialects that it does not have in Standard English. In Standard English it occurs as the negation of *are*, as in *we aren't, you aren't, they aren't*. Interestingly, it also occurs as the negative of the question-form *am I?* = *aren't I?* In Standard English, however, the negative of the statement-form *I am* has to be *I'm not*, but in some Nonstandard Dialects *I aren't* can occur.

Another interesting and widespread form is the use of *never* as a way of making past-tense verb forms negative. In many Nonstandard Dialects, *never* can refer to a single occasion, whereas in Standard English it has to refer to an extended period or to repeated occasions. Thus we find:

Standard English	Nonstandard Dialects
I didn't do it	I never done it
You didn't break it?	You never broke it?

Expressions such as *She seen him yesterday but she never today* are common.

As far as Traditional Dialects are concerned, interesting negative verb forms are widely found in the Staffordshire area. These are forms of *shan't, won't, can't*, etc., which are formed from *no* rather than from *not*. Thus *shan't* is *shanno* or *shanna* and *didn't* is *didno* or *didna*. In the Potteries one can hear:

> Cost lend us a quid? No, I conna =
> 'Can you (canst thou) lend me a pound? No, I can't'

and

> I anna done it = 'I haven't done it'

Even in Standard English there is variation. As we saw in chapter 1, people from the north of England are more likely to say *I'll not do it*,

I've not done it, whereas people from the south of England are more likely to say *I won't do it*, *I haven't done it*.

FORMS OF *BE*

The verb *to be* in English is highly irregular, and most dialects have forms which differ from Standard English at least in some respects. Some, for instance, have *was* throughout the past tense – *you was, we was, they was* – while others have generalized *were* – *I were, she were*. Yet others distinguish between positive *was* and negative *were*:

> He was there, weren't he?
> You was there, weren't you?

Even more interesting is the amount of variation found in the present tense, corresponding to Standard English *am, are, is*. Some Traditional Dialects in the North, for instance, have *is* for all persons, while others in the Staffordshire area have *am* throughout. Yet others have *be* or *bin* or *are*. Traditional Dialects of the 1950s and 1960s show the pattern illustrated in map 23 for the form *am I*. The overall division is as follows:

Northumberland	*am*
Lower North	*is*
Lancashire	*am*
Staffordshire	*bin/am*
Eastern Central	*am*
Western Southwest	*be*
Northern Southwest	*bin/be*
Eastern Southwest	*be*
Berkshire	*be*
Sussex	*be*
Kent and Surrey	*are*
Essex	*am*
Eastern Counties	*am*
Northamptonshire and Cambridgeshire	*are*

The standard form *I am* thus occurs in a contiguous region comprising East Anglia, Lincolnshire, Leicestershire, South Yorkshire and

Map 23 *Am I*

Lancashire. There is then a gap for the Lower North, which has *I is*, with *I am* resuming in the North (and on into Scotland). This division has sometimes been explained as an intrusion into the Lower North of *is* as a Scandinavian form, and certainly the Lower North was an area of very high Viking Norwegian and Danish settlement. In the same region, for instance, *till* is still used in the meaning *to*, which it also has in the modern Scandinavian languages:

Standard English:	They sent us to London
Lower North:	They sent us till London
Norwegian:	Dei sende oss til London

The Future

It is probably true to say that grammatical differences between the Modern Dialects are not so numerous as differences between the Traditional Dialects. It is unlikely, however, that the differences that remain will now further diminish in number to any great extent. We saw in chapter 3 that accent differences will continue to remain with us, as innovations continually begin life in particular areas and subsequently spread to other regions, leading to new patterns of regional differentiation. The same thing is likely to be true of grammar, although the trend towards conformity is perhaps a little stronger here. Variation among the Modern Dialects at the grammatical level is certainly still rich and considerable, and happily this diversity seems likely to remain with us as a source of interest, colour and enjoyment for the foreseeable future, in spite of the efforts of those in the media and the educational system who would like to see an increase in conformity and uniformity.

5

♦

Dialect Words

It is a matter of common observation that the shoes that children wear
at school for activities such as physical education, folk-dancing and
sport are known by different names in different parts of the British
Isles. In spite of the recent introduction of new styles and commercial
names such as *trainers*, regional dialect variation still survives for these
particular items of clothing, as map 24 shows. It is true that, even
before the advent of *trainers*, non-regional names such as *gymshoes* were
available. But actually most speakers seem to have used, or at least
known, one of the regional words instead or as well. If you went to
school in Newcastle you call these shoes *sandshoes*. If you went to
school in Liverpool you call them *gollies*, and in Bristol they are known
as *daps*. In Nottingham people call them *pumps*, while in London they
are *plimsolls*. *Sandshoes* is also used in Scotland and Australia, while
daps is also used in much of Wales. In Ireland, they are called
whiteslippers in Dublin and *gutties* in Belfast.

Regional Vocabulary

In the rest of this book we have divided England up into Traditional
Dialect and Modern Dialect areas – with warnings about the rather
fuzzy and arbitrary nature of these divisions – on the basis of pronunciation and grammar. Vocabulary differentiation, too, relates to these
areas. This regional variation in the words for *gymshoe* is a feature
which relates rather clearly to the division of Modern Dialects into
areas that we made on the basis of accents in chapter 3. Thus *sandshoes*
is the word found in our Northeast area, while *gollies* is found in our
Merseyside area. *Daps* found in the Central and Northern Southwest

Map 24 *Gymshoes*

areas, *pumps* in the Central North and Central areas, and *plimsolls* in the East Anglia, South Midlands, and Home Counties and Lower South-west areas.

However, we have to admit that there is much more regional variation in words used in Traditional Dialects than there is at the level of Modern Dialects. In the Traditional Dialects, we find that some words are typical of our small sub-areas, while others are characteristic of the larger Traditional Dialect divisions that we established in chapter 2. For instance, the whole of the North Traditional Dialect area (the Lower North and Northumberland) shares the term *pace-egg* = 'Easter egg', from Middle English *pasch* = 'Easter' (originally from the Old French *pasche*). These dialects all also have *whin* = 'gorse' from Old Norse. The whole of the Western area, on the other hand (the Northern Southwest, Western Southwest, Eastern Southwest and Southeast), has *wops* rather than the *wasp* found elsewhere.

If we look at the country generally, we can notice the following association of words with particular Traditional Dialect areas. (We give only a few examples to illustrate the point – many scores of others could have been cited.) For instance, two words typical of the dialect of Northumberland (and Scotland) are *to stot*, meaning 'to bounce' as of a ball (the origin of this word is not known); and *poke* = 'bag', which is either from Old French *poque* or Old Norse *poki* = 'pouch'. A word associated mainly with the Lower North area, on the other hand, is the verb *to wark*, meaning 'to ache', from the Old English word *wærcan*. In our more detailed subdivisions of the Lower North, we find further that *to grave* = 'to dig' is typical of the Cumbria area, while *pincer-toed* and *pincher-toed* = 'pigeon-toed' are typical of North Yorkshire and Durham, and East Yorkshire respectively.

Moving down into the Central dialect area, we can see that words typical of the Lancashire area include *mazy* = 'dizzy/giddy', which is related to *amazed* and is from Old English *amasian* = 'to bewilder'; and *kay-handed* = 'left-handed' (from Scandinavian). Typical Staffordshire area words are *mussrow* = 'fieldmouse' (= mouse + shrew), and *splint* = 'splinter', from mediaeval Dutch *splinte*, compare Modern Dutch *splinter*.

In Eastern Central dialects, typical words from the South Yorkshire area include *tab* = 'ear' and *spice* = 'sweets'. Words usual mainly in the Lincolnshire Traditional Dialect area include *to pelt* = 'to throw' and *maddocks* = 'maggots' from Old Norse *maðkr* (which is also the source of the more deviant Standard English *maggots*), compare modern Norwegian *maddik*. Leicestershire words include *to yack* = 'to throw' and *snath* = 'scythe-handle', from Anglo-Saxon *snæd*.

In the Southern dialect area, we can note that typical Eastern Counties words include *push* = 'pimple, boil', which is from mediaeval Dutch or Low German – the modern Dutch word is *puist*; and *dicky* = 'donkey'. This last word is interesting as it is simply the familiar form of the man's name Richard, like the Northern dialect word *cuddy*, from Cuthbert, and the Central, Southern and Standard English word *donkey*, from Duncan. The East Central dialect area shows *stunt* = 'steep' and *sludder* = 'mud'.

In the Western Traditional Dialect area, a number of words also stand out as being typical of certain regions. In the Northern Southwest we find *quist* = 'pigeons' and *gibbons* = 'spring onions'; and in the Eastern Southwest *chimmock* 'chimney' and *hen-toed* 'pigeon-toed'. In the Western Southwest we can find *granfer* for 'grandfather', and *chibboles* = 'spring onions' from Old French *cibole* – compare modern French *ciboule* = 'chives'; while words associated with smaller sub-areas include Devon and Cornwall *rummage* = 'rubbish', and Somerset and Dorset *upover* = 'upstairs'. In the Southeast, distinctive Traditional Dialect words include *bread-crock* = 'bread-bin', from Old English *crocc* = 'pot'; and *spean* = 'prong of a fork'.

We should also note that dialects vary not only in having different words for the same things or activities or ideas. They may also differ in the words they use for expressing emotional states and intensity of feeling. For example, the Standard English word *very* also occurs in Nonstandard Dialects, but most of these dialects have in addition other words which can also be used as intensifiers. In Traditional Dialects, for instance, corresponding to the Standard English sentence

It's very tasty

we might find

It's gey tasty (Northumberland)
It's gradely tasty (Lancashire)
That's wholly tasty (Eastern Counties)
It be main tasty (Wiltshire and Hampshire).

In Modern Dialects we also find

It's right tasty (Central North)
It's well tasty (Home Counties)

Dialects also differ regionally in the vocabulary they use for addressing different people. Terms of address which are used in different parts of the country, and in particular situations, include *love, dear, ducks, mate, john, tosh, jimmy* and so on. In the Northeast *hinnie* is used, while in Eastern Counties Traditional Dialect *bor* is a frequent term of address. Each of these terms has rules associated with them as to who can say them and who they can say them to. These rules usually have to do with the age, sex and degree of acquaintance of the speaker and hearer. Consider who if anyone you might address as *love*, and who might and might not address you in this way, and how you would feel about it if they did. These rules differ as between different regional and social dialects. Even where terms of address are the same in different areas, rules for who can call who what may be different. Thus in most parts of England there is a restriction on the use of the term *dear* such that men may not use this term to each other. For some Devon and Cornwall Traditional Dialect speakers, however, this restriction does not apply, and it is quite normal therefore to hear one man greet another with 'Hello, m'dearr!.'

Dialect and Standard Words

In the case of gymshoes, as we saw, each region of the country has a word which is confined to that particular region. Most cases of dialect variation, however, are not like this. In most cases there is a nonregional word which is used by Standard English speakers throughout the country which is also the local dialect word in one particular area. This is because, where regional vocabulary variation existed in the centuries before the development of Standard English, one word from one of the Traditional Dialects usually became the Standard English word, with the other variants remaining characteristic only of regional dialects. In the Traditional Dialect area in question, therefore, there will only be one word, while everywhere else there will be two – the local dialect word and the standard word.

In many cases, the word which became the Standard English word was taken from one of the Southeastern Traditional Dialects. This can be seen from map 25, which shows the local dialect word for *ear* in Traditional Dialects. In the south of England, the dialect word is also the Standard English word, *ear*, while in the north and the Eastern Counties the dialect word is *lug*, and in the South Yorkshire area the word is *tab*. In most of the north of England, then, two words are used, either dialect *lug* or standard *ear*, while in the south only one word is available since both Standard English speakers and dialect speakers use *ear*.

This is all because Standard English started life as a regional dialect from the southeast of England, and it therefore often happens that the

Map 25   *Ear*

Traditional Dialects from this part of the country coincide in vocabulary with Standard English. But this does not always mean that it is only the southeastern dialects that have contributed to the vocabulary of Standard English. Map 26 for *hungry*, for instance, shows that along the south coast and in the Southwest and Western Central areas, words unknown in Standard English are used in Traditional Dialects: *thirl*, *leery*, *clammed*; while for *something*, the Traditional Dialects of the Eastern Counties and Northumberland agree with Standard English

114

Map 26 *Hungry*

and the Southeast, whereas other areas have *summat*.

There are also, interestingly, quite a number of cases where the Traditional Dialects have words which have *no* counterpart in Standard English at all – where the Traditional Dialects have words for objects or concepts which do not exist in the Modern Dialects, and where, therefore, we can say that none of the variants available has made it into the standard. This relative richness of dialect vocabulary can be explained by the association of Standard English with middle-class, educated urban

115

people who had no experience of phenomena familiar to people living and working in rural occupations. It is difficult, for example, to think of Standard English words corresponding to Devon and Cornwall *atchett* = 'pole slung across a stream to stop cattle passing', or *smitch* = 'dirty smoke from a fire'; or Northern Southwest *bracking* = 'the chipping of eggshells when hatching begins', or *wane* = 'the side of a plank which is not quite rectangular because it has been cut from the side of the trunk'.

Vocabulary Origins

The variety of vocabulary in the Traditional Dialects of England is enormous – Joseph Wright's *English Dialect Dictionary*, for instance, published around the turn of the century, comes in six very large volumes. But where did all these different words come from in the first place? What are the reasons for the development of regional variation in vocabulary?

One explanation is that, at least in a few instances, the differences *have always been there*. This is the case, as far as we can tell, with the northern word *oxter* = 'armpit' (see map 27) When we say that the difference has always been there, what we of course mean is that it has been there ever since English has been spoken in Britain. The English language, or its ancestor, was brought to Britain in the fourth, fifth and sixth centuries by raiders, mercenaries, invaders and eventually settlers from the North Sea coasts stretching from what is now the Netherlands to what is now Denmark. The Germanic dialects they brought with them – which were the ancestors of Dutch and Frisian as well as English – were already then differentiated according to where on the North Sea coast they came from. It is possible, although we are not entirely sure about this, that the Angles, who seem to have settled in areas from southeastern Scotland down to East Anglia, were from the coast of Denmark, while the Saxons, who came from what is now North Germany settled further south, from Essex to the West Country (hence Essex = East Saxons, Sussex = South Saxons, Wessex = West Saxons). The other Germanic peoples who invaded Britain and for whom we have names are the Jutes (from modern Jutland, Denmark) and the Frisians (from the shores of what now is the Netherlands and northwest Germany).

In some cases, then, settlement patterns led to dialect differences

116

Map 27 *Armpit*

from the continent being transplanted to Britain. Our earliest records
of Anglo-Saxon or Old English, from several centuries after the invasions, show considerable regional variation in vocabulary and in pronunciation. Some of these differences would have arisen in the centuries
after settlement, but others may have been brought with them from the
continent by the invading tribes. In any case, already in the Anglo-
Saxon period, we see the word *oxta* = modern *oxter* confined to the
same northern area of Britain where we still find it today.

117

In other cases, however, other explanations for regional differences in vocabulary are required. It often happens, for instance, that geographical patterns of dialect variation are due to the replacement in a particular area of an older, long-established word by a newer, incoming one. In some cases, as we shall see below, the newer word is a Standard English word which replaces a word confined to Traditional Dialect. However, even in the centuries before Standard English existed – before there was any such concept, which is to say up until the seventeenth or eighteenth centuries – the same phenomenon still occurred.

For example, the word *autumn* is normal in the Traditional Dialects of the Eastern Counties, the Central East, the Southeast, and the Northern Southwest. On the other hand, in the Western Southwest, the Eastern Southwest and in the Lincolnshire area, the normal word is *fall*. This reflects the introduction into England in late mediaeval times, and only *partial* acceptance of, the originally French word *autumn*, compare modern French *automne*. (Thousands of other French words were of course also introduced after the Norman conquest.) This eventually replaced the original Anglo-Saxon word *fall* in Standard English in England and in some of the dialects, but by no means all of them. It is clear that at one time the use of *autumn* must have been much less widespread than it is today, since the form which was carried by settlers to the United States, and which is still the Standard English word there, was *fall*. Interestingly, the whole of the Central area (except Lincolnshire) and the Northern Traditional Dialect area have yet another word: *backend*. (In Scotland, this word is still used even by Modern Dialect speakers.)

The other language, in addition to French, which has also been particularly influential in the growth of geographical patterns of variation in English dialects is Old Norse – the direct ancestor of the modern Scandinavian languages Norwegian, Swedish, Danish, Icelandic and Faroese. Old Norse influence on the English language was quite considerable. Many words now used in *all* English dialects, such as *they*, *egg*, *skirt*, are of Scandinavian origin.

However, the heaviest Scandinavian linguistic influence seems to have been on the dialects of the Lower North. This area was quite heavily colonized by Vikings – Norwegians coming mostly from the west, often via Ireland, and Danes from the east, especially from the ninth century onwards. This led to at least 200 years of Scandinavian-English bilingualism in many places. (At that time, however, Old Norse

Map 28   *To play*

and Old English were very much more similar than their descendant languages are today.)

The extent of this influence on the Lower North can be seen from map 28, giving Traditional Dialect words for the verb *to play*. Here the intrusion of Scandinavian *lake* or *laik* (corresponding to modern Norwegian *leike*) can be clearly seen, dividing the original English *play* area into two. *Laik* is still used by many Modern Dialect speakers, especially in Yorkshire.

119

Map 29   *Child*

Similar patterns can be seen for *lop* (modern Norwegian *loppe*) = 'flea', and *nieve* (modern Norwegian *neve*) = 'fist'. Map 29 shows a much larger area than just the Lower North for the word *bairn* (modern Norwegian *barn*) = 'child', which also extends on up into Scotland, as is well known. It is possible in fact that this word once covered the whole of the original Danelaw area. It was certainly used by old Traditional Dialect speakers in Norfolk in the 1930s, and currently seems to be receding northwards.

French and Scandinavian influence on English dialects are the result of the Norman and Viking invasions respectively. The influence of Cornish and Welsh is of a rather different sort. Cornish and Welsh were originally the same language, which was spoken all over England and Wales and much of Scotland before the Anglo-Saxon invasions. A very few Welsh words survive in Standard English (*brock* = 'badger', *bannock* = 'cake', *tor* = 'peak', *coomb* = 'valley'), but in certain dialects there is rather more influence. Parts of Herefordshire and Shropshire, for instance, were Welsh-speaking until very recently (indeed, there are still some Welsh speakers left in some areas), and dialects of the Northern Southwest show some vocabulary influence from Welsh, such as *tallet* = 'hayloft' from Welsh *taflawd*. Most words of Cornish origin are found only in the English dialect of Cornwall, e.g. *crouse* or *croust* = 'snack' from Cornish *crowst* (originally from Old French *crouste*), and *clicky-handed* from Old Cornish *glikin* (also found in western Devon).

The Cockney dialect is also of course famous for its distinctive vocabulary. Some of it has its origins in types of speaker creativity such as backslang, like *yob* from *boy*, or rhyming slang, like *cobblers* = 'rubbish' from *cobblers' awls* = *balls*. Other words have been borrowed from the Gypsy language Romany, such as *pal* = 'friend' (= 'brother' in Romany), *cosh* from Romany *koshter* = 'stick', and *mush*, which is a term of address in Cockney but is actually from the Anglo-Romany word *moosh* = 'man'. However, a lot of Cockney words have also come from the East European Jewish language Yiddish, which is itself derived from mediaeval German. Originally Yiddish words in Cockney include *shtook* = 'financial trouble' and *gelt* = 'money'. Words which have made their way from Yiddish via Cockney into the standard language, albeit at the level of slang, include *gezump* (now mostly *gazump*) = 'swindle' and *nosh* = 'food' – compare modern German *naschen* = 'to nibble'.

Vocabulary Loss

We have noted that variation between the words used by different dialects is decreasing. Variation between the Modern Dialects at the level of vocabulary remains, as we have seen in the case of *plimsoll/ sandshoe* etc., but, sadly for those who are fond of variety and richness in vocabulary, it is clear that there is much less differentiation between

Modern Dialect words than between Traditional Dialect words. What we are witnessing in the modern English language – while, as we have seen, variation in accents remains or even grows – is an ever-increasing uniformity at the level of vocabulary. Fewer people know fewer Traditional Dialect words, and the words themselves are confined to narrower and narrower functions and to smaller and smaller geographical areas. Very many dialect words are gradually being lost from the language, as rural life-styles change, and as the Modern Dialects replace the Traditional Dialects.

For instance, a study was carried out in the Cumbrian area of the Lower North in the 1970s into knowledge of Traditional Dialect words such as *yat* = 'gate' (which is a form occurring throughout the Lower North, and can also be found, for example, in the Northern South-west); *to laik* = 'play'; and *to loup* = 'jump'. This showed that a much smaller percentage of junior-school children in a small town in Cumberland used such words in 1975 than in 1960.

Similarly, a study was carried out in Norwich into knowledge of Eastern Counties dialect words by people of different ages. Work in 1968 and again in 1983 showed that people's knowledge of Eastern Counties Traditional Dialect vocabulary was declining very dramatically. Everybody born before 1900 used – or had used at some time in their lives – words such as *mawther* = 'girl' and *dwile* = 'floorcloth' and knew very well what they meant. People born between 1900 and 1930 all knew what such words meant, but only some of them used them, while only some speakers born between 1930 and 1960 were familiar with the words. Young people born after 1960 had for the most part never even heard such words, and none of them knew what they meant.

The potential loss of words should not be underestimated. The richness of Traditional Dialect vocabulary is very considerable. Just consider briefly the number of different words for 'pod' (as of peas) uncovered by the *Survey of English Dialects*: hull, swad, shull, husk, shell, cosh, shuck, pod. Or the different words for '*throw*': throw, heave, train, fling, chuck, hull, cop, yack, pelt, cob, clod, scop, troy, swail.

It is interesting, however, to note that some types of Traditional Dialect word are more likely to be lost than other types. One thing that the Norwich survey showed was that young people do continue to know and use certain Traditional Dialect words, including the word *squit* = 'nonsense'. (*Squit*, incidentally, is also known and used by Traditional Dialect speakers as far away as Herefordshire, but is not used by Standard English speakers in this meaning.) *Squit* is a word which is used in informal situations in order to, for example, disparage something that someone has just said, and has survived so far quite strongly in Norwich. Most people in Norwich still know the word and use it, even though they are Modern Dialect and not Traditional Dialect speakers. The reason for this is that the word is used informally, maybe jokingly, and is therefore not necessarily in competition with Standard English words such as *nonsense* which can be used in more formal situations.

Mawther, on the other hand, was originally the stylistically neutral Eastern Counties Traditional Dialect word for 'girl'. That is, it was used in formal and serious as well as in informal and light-hearted circumstances, and as such it was in direct competition with the more widespread and Standard English word *girl*, which has now almost totally replaced it, at least in the city of Norwich. It is true that some of the Norwich people born after 1960 may come to learn this word later in life, but they are unlikely to ever *use* it as their normal word for 'girl'. The fate of the word *mawther*, in fact, is typical of what happens to many Traditional Dialect words which are in competition with other words which also happen to be the Standard English words.

Map 30 shows, in fact, that when the *Survey of English Dialects* work was carried out in the 1950s and 1960s, there were five words for 'girl' that had widespread currency in the Traditional Dialects. Today we can say that only two of these, *girl* and *lass*, survive with any vitality in the Modern Dialects. The loss of variety and the increase in uniformity is clear:

Traditional Dialects:	girl, lass, mawther, maiden, wench,
Modern Dialects:	girl, lass
Standard English:	girl

The word *mawther* is now known only to older people in Norfolk and Suffolk, but very few of them actually use it except as a joke. The word *maiden* is known to most English speakers as an archaic word that occurs, for example, in folk-songs and in a few fossilized usages, such as a *maiden over* in cricket. (In some dialects it also means a clothes-horse.) *Wench* is also known by most English speakers, but is hardly ever used except jokingly and with a very restricted range of meanings, e.g. for a lusty young woman in a mediaeval setting. And *lass*, which at the moment survives quite strongly in the north of England as a word corresponding to *girl* and *daughter*, nevertheless is quite likely –

Map 30   *Girl*

although not certain – also to become reduced in use and meaning. This is already the case in southern England, where *lass* is certainly understood, but is not used unless with very restricted meaning. Incidentally, the history of these five words is as follows:

girl: The origin of this word is not known. Our first record of its use dates only from about the year 1200 onwards.

lass: We have no record of this word being used before about 1300. It is

124

probably of Scandinavian origin, but we can't be quite sure about this.

mawther: Nobody is sure what the origin of this word is either, but it is thought to be possibly of Scandinavian origin. Some people have pointed out its similarity to *mother*, and have observed that in Norwegian dialects it is still very common to call little girls *mor* = 'mother'. Our first record of this word is from about 1450.

maiden: This is an Anglo-Saxon word of considerable antiquity, and has probably been used for as long as English has been spoken.

wench: This word has been used to mean 'girl' probably only from about 1300, but it appears to be derived from the Anglo-Saxon word *wencel*, which meant 'child'.

Increasingly, then, we are seeing a process of **lexical attrition** – the eating away of dialect words – in the dialects of England. As we have said, differences remain in the Modern Dialects, including even within Standard English in some cases, but more and more often these differences are becoming confined to certain domestic and/or informal areas of social life, such as food and drink, clothing and children's games.

For example, it is well known that people in different parts of the country have different names for preparing a pot of tea. In some places they *make* tea, in others they *mash* it, in yet others they *mask* it, *wet* it or *brew* it. And the tea itself, while we are waiting for it to be ready to drink, *brews*, *steeps*, *stews* or *infuses*, depending on where it is.

Beer, too, can be called by different names in different parts of the country, and combinations of different types of beer are a particularly rich source of regional vocabulary differences, though even here nationwide advertising and commercial pressures are also leading to lexical attrition. For example, a pint of mild and bitter mixed together goes by various names. In East Anglia – Colchester, Ipswich, Norwich – its usual name was *a pint of twos*, but fewer and fewer people know this as the drink itself becomes less usual and populations become more mobile.

Another area of modern life where different words survive for the same object in different parts of the country in the Modern Dialects is that of words for bread and cakes, where these are made, advertised and sold locally rather than nationally. For instance, what some call a *roll*, others call a *bun*, or a *cob*, or a *bap*, or a *bannock*, while in other areas more than one of these words is used with different meanings for each.

And another good example of vocabulary variation in Modern Dialects is provided by the word *splinter* – a thin piece of wood that you may get stuck in your finger. Again because this word is from a domestic, informal and non-commercial area of life, regional variation survives here even in the case of people who do not speak Traditional Dialect. In addition to *splinter*, other words still in current use include *shiver, sliver, speel, spell, spoal, spile, spill, spelk* and *splint. Splinter, splint* (Staffordshire), *spill* (Northern Southwest) and *spile* (Lancashire) are of Dutch origin. *Speel* (Cumbria) and *spoal* (South Yorkshire) are Scandinavian, while *shiver* (Norfolk), *sliver* (Essex and Suffolk) and *spelk* (Northumberland) are from Old English.

Also particularly rich in regional variation is the vocabulary of children's games, in so far as these are not part of a nationwide official or television-based culture. Map 31 is based on a famous study conducted by Iona and Peter Opie into truce-words used by children in different parts of the country when they want to take time out from a game. It shows that there is considerable diversity in the words used, including *keys, barley, skinch, exes, fainites, scribs* and *cree.*

The overall picture, then, is one of retreat for words which are not recognized as Standard English – retreat into informal and jocular usage, and into local and domestic areas of life. This retreat, however, also has a geographical dimension. We can illustrate this clearly with a number of examples. Firstly, the word *mawther* = 'girl', which we have already discussed. We know that it was formerly used over a rather wider area than it has been in more recent times, and its geographical shrinkage can be plotted as follows:

1850 Norfolk, Suffolk, Essex, Cambridgeshire,
     Hertfordshire
1900 Norfolk, Suffolk, Essex, Cambridgeshire
1925 Norfolk, Suffolk
1950 East Norfolk, East Suffolk
1975 no longer in widespread use

That is to say that this particular word has been more and more confined, like many other such words, to a geographically peripheral area of the country, as it is ousted by a word which neighbouring dialects share with Standard English.

Map 32 shows a similar case. Traditional Dialect words corresponding to Standard English *to dig* include *to dig, to delve* and *to grave.* We

Map 31   Children's truce terms

happen to know that *dig* is a newer word than the others in the history
of the English language, not having appeared until mediaeval times as
a loan-word from French *diguer* = 'to dig a ditch'. But the map clearly
shows that now nearly all the Traditional Dialects of England use *dig*,
with *delve* and *grave*, as it were, having been pushed to the geographical
edges of the country. *Delve*, of course, does survive in Standard
English usage, but only in the metaphorical sense of, for instance,
delving into a problem.

127

Map 32   *To dig*

A similar, if more complicated picture emerges from map 27 (p. 117) for *armpit*. This map reveals an interesting historical progression. The North uses the ancient word *oxter* (as does Scotland), as we saw above. In the rest of the country, however, the geographical patterning strongly suggests that at one time the whole central part of the country used to have the word *armhole*, but that the word *armpit*, which is also of course the Standard English word, has gradually thrust northwards, separating one *armhole* area from another and leaving behind what

Map 33   *Bridge*

dialectologists call **relic areas** or isolated islands with the older form, like the one we can see in the Bedfordshire–Buckinghamshire–Hertfordshire area.

Again, map 33, which shows Traditional Dialect words for *bridge*, indicates that the southern area of England has the original Anglo-Saxon word *bridge*, while the northern area has the originally Scandinavian Old Norse word *brig*. The geographical patterning of the occurrence of

129

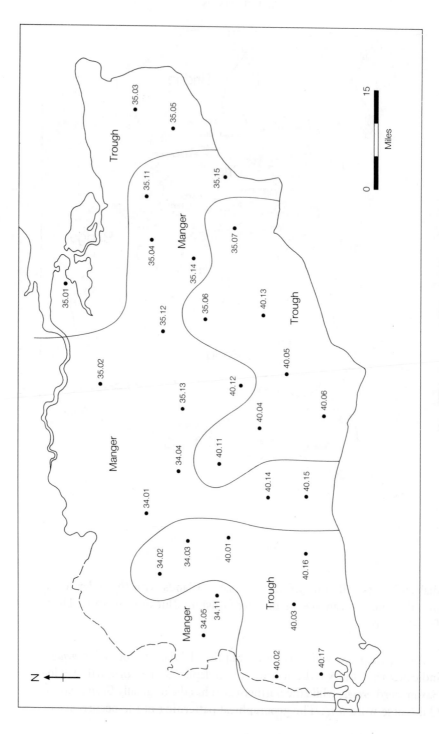

Map 34 Distribution of words for *Trough* (in cow-house) in *Survey of English Dialects* materials; 34.01 etc. = dialect localities investigated

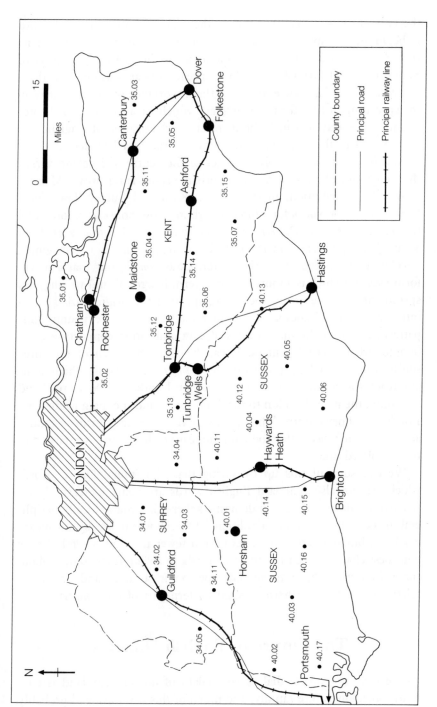

Map 35 Main routes in Surrey, Kent and Sussex

the two words suggests that the southern and Standard English word is beginning to spread north, and in a rather interesting way. In its spread northwards, *bridge* has first invaded the coastal city areas of Sunderland and Grimsby, and then spread outwards again from these centres. This is just one example of the importance of urban centres in the spreading of new forms in language which we also noted in chapter 3, and of the way in which the increasing urbanization of England has contributed in this century to the loss of Traditional Dialects.

And it is not only simply a matter of the centre of England versus the geographical periphery, or of urban versus rural areas. Map 34 shows the distribution, in the Sussex, Kent and Surrey Traditional Dialect areas, of words for a food-trough in a cow-house as recorded by the *Survey of English Dialects*. It cannot be the case that *trough* has been adopted independently in three different areas. Rather, we imagine a development whereby the original form was *trough*, but that a newer form *manger* (which is a more standard term in agricultural writing) has spread into the area from the north, splitting the original *trough* area into three. Map 35 goes some considerable way towards explaining this pattern. It shows the main routes of communication connecting London to urban coastal centres. It can be seen that each of the three southward-encroaching prongs of the *manger* area, two of which actually reach the coast, coincide with the main London to Dover road and rail route, the main London to Brighton route, and the main route from London to Portsmouth. The spread of the incoming form is clearly accelerated in areas with good communications links, and is retarded in more isolated areas.

We can sum all this up by saying that Traditional Dialect words which are not also Standard English words are being increasingly restricted to informal usages in domestic spheres in geographically peripheral areas of the country. Traditional Dialect words are by no means dead yet, but they are getting fewer and fewer in number, and already your best chance of hearing them is to talk in an informal context about some domestic subject to an older person in a rural, and preferably relatively isolated, northern or southwestern part of the country.

The Future of English Dialects

As we have noted, the dialect vocabulary of modern England is currently shrinking quite rapidly, and much of this diversity will probably eventually disappear. This is likely to be compensated for to a certain extent by the growth of new accents and the development of new patterns of Modern Dialect variation at the level of pronunciation and, maybe, grammar. But what about the vocabulary of English dialects? Exactly why is it being lost? And does it matter if the Traditional Dialect words do disappear?

As far as the reasons for lexical attrition are concerned, we have touched on some of them already. Many local dialect words have to do with the rural way of life and, especially, with non-mechanized farming techniques. As this way of life, and these techniques, disappear, so will the words that go with them. The *Survey of English Dialects*, for instance, discovered a wealth of words to describe the act of putting sheaves of corn together in a field for drying: *hiling, shocking, shucking, stacking, sticking, stitching, stocking, stooking, stowking* and *thraving*. Now that nobody does this anymore, the words themselves will eventually be forgotten.

Loss of this technological sort would appear to be inevitable, and is, as it were, often repaired in part by the introduction of new technical vocabularies. Much lexical attrition, however, is the result of rather more complicated processes. When, for example, articles for sale are made by nationwide or multinational companies and advertised in national newspapers or, more particularly, on national television, there will be a strong tendency to uniformity in the vocabulary that goes with these objects. To the extent that local shops and companies remain in business, on the other hand, local words will have a stronger chance of survival. It is unlikely, for instance, that the dialect diversity apparent in the use in different parts of the country of words such as *bullets, cooshies, goodies, follies, pops, spice, sucks, suckers* and *toffees* will survive the television advertising of sweets or even American *candy*. On the other hand, to the extent that local family butchers continue to prepare and sell their wares locally, *chitterlings* are likely to be called *chitlins*, or *hides*, or *knotlings*, or *link-hides*, or *puddings*, or *small-puddings*, or *ropps*, depending on what part of the country they are being sold in.

There is little that can be done about the lexical attrition that accompanies these two processes. Nor can we fight against the increased geographical mobility that has come with better transport facilities, and the loss of regional diversity that this brings with it. Nor would we want to fight against the increased educational opportunities that have become available this century, with all children in the country being exposed to the Standard English dialect. It is possible to argue, however, that it is nevertheless important to fight for the preservation of regional vocabulary, as far as we can, as well as for the preservation of regional pronunciation and grammar.

It is true that, in our not entirely egalitarian society, it is unfortunately still considered to be acceptable to discriminate against people, especially young people, on the grounds of their dialect, in a way that would now be unthinkable on the grounds of their race or their sex. That is why we have to give all children in this country the chance to learn to write Standard English at school, so that they can guard themselves against this form of discrimination.

It is equally true, however, that English speakers should be encouraged to be more tolerant towards the dialects of others, and to feel free to use and preserve their own dialects if they wish. The Traditional Dialects and Modern Dialects of England are part of our linguistic environment, and should be protected, just as our physical environment should be protected. Very few people would be happy if the whole of England ended up resembling Milton Keynes, excellent place as Milton Keynes is in its way. This would make our country a very dull and unstimulating place to live in. The same is true of our dialects, and of the local cultures that go with them. If everyone in this country spoke the same dialect, and used the same words, it would become a less enjoyable and interesting place. Just imagine if Liverpudlians sounded exactly like Cockneys! Or if you couldn't tell an English person from a Scot! Of course, very occasionally, dialect differences can give rise to comprehension difficulties – the more unlike your dialect someone else's dialect is, the more difficult they will be to understand. But difficulties of this type in England are very rarely at all serious, and the solution to them, where they do occur, is not to bully everyone into speaking Standard English or Cockney, but for us all to improve our abilities, and our good will, as listeners. Very often, it must be admitted, people do not understand because they do not want to.

There is also the further danger that, if everyone in the country spoke in the same way, and shared exactly the same vocabulary, they would start thinking in the same way too, and come to share exactly the same values. In a small and relatively homogeneous country like England, there is already a good deal of cultural uniformity and social cohesion, which has sometimes in our history proved to be a source of strength. But a rapid decrease in what diversity we still have could lead to cultural stagnation, and a reduction in opportunities for cultural and social progress. It is a good thing that Geordies and Cockneys and

Scousers, northerners and midlanders and southerners, are somewhat different sorts of people, and have different ideas, values and cultures. The fact that they speak different dialects helps them to stay that way. If we were all to end up speaking, thinking and behaving the same, we would eventually be left with only a single monolithic English culture that would greatly reduce our chances in the future of exploring alternative ideas, and of looking at alternative ways of making progress for our society. This is a further reason why the preservation of dialect differences should be fought for. Dialect differences both symbolize and help to preserve local identities and individual ways of looking at the world.

The preservation of dialect diversity should therefore be encouraged. It is true that all dialects of all languages have always been subject to change, and that words are always dying out and new ones being created. What we are seeing now, however, is something different. We are seeing a strong trend towards the growth of uniformity. If the levelling out of dialect differences through processes such as lexical attrition is to be slowed down, it will be necessary to encourage speakers to continue to speak their own dialects by cultivating *pride* in these dialects and their vocabularies. It is therefore important for speakers to recognize that, although Standard English is an extremely important means of communication in the country and the world, it is not linguistically superior to any other dialect, and that there is nothing to be ashamed of in speaking local, Nonstandard Dialects.

Other European countries such as Norway and Switzerland have shown that it is perfectly possible to develop modern, democratic and technologically advanced societies in which the vast majority of the population speak regional dialects, and are proud to do so. We can learn from the pride these peoples take in the use and preservation of their individual, local ways of speaking, and the way in which their governments and educational systems do not attempt to impose national linguistic conformity.

Londoners may move into our villages and laugh at us because we are not 'sophisticated' enough to say *floorcloth* instead of *dwile*. School-teachers may say that it is 'wrong' to say *loup* and 'right' to say *jump*. But if we desire to continue to fight against lexical attrition, and loss of dialects generally, we will try to resist pressures such as these, and, if we have enough patience, attempt to persuade such people to see the error of their ways so that they may become more linguistically tolerant human beings.

The different forms taken by the English language in modern England represent the results of 1,500 years of linguistic and cultural development. It is in the nature of language, and in the nature of society, that these dialects will always be changing. The fact, however, that many of them are in many respects currently all changing in the same direction has to be viewed with concern. English has never been a monolithic language, spoken in the same way by people everywhere, and it never will be. But unless we can rid ourselves of the idea that speaking anything other than Standard English is a sign of ignorance and lack of 'sophistication', much of what linguistic richness and diversity remains in the English language in this country may be lost.

Notes

◆

Chapter 1 Language Variety in England

1 H. V. Morton, *In Search of England*, London: Methuen, 1927.
2 Linton Kwesi Johnson, *Inglan is a Bitch*, London: Race Today Publications, 1981.
3 *The Kushti Bokkengro*, London: Scripture Gift Mission, Eccleston Street, London SW1 [no date].

Chapter 2 The Pronunciation of Traditional Dialects

1 Robert Burns, 'Auld Lang Syne', in W. Beattie and H. Meikle (eds), *Robert Burns*, London: Penguin, 1946.
2 J. Relph, 'The Amourous Maiden', in *Westmoreland Poems* [no editor], London: J. R. Smith, 1839.
3 From *Tales and Ballads of Wearside*.
4 Syd Bloomfield, 'Strangers', in L. Reeves (ed.), *The Harvester I*, 1975 (Mooney Publications) [Folded after 2 issues]; taken from M. Wakelin, *The Southwest of England*, Amsterdam: Benjamins, 1986.
5 Mabel Peacock, 'The Lincolnshire Poacher', *c*.1890; taken from G. E. Campion, *Lincolnshire Dialects*, Boston, Lincs.: Richard Kay, 20 Sleaford Rd. [no date].
6 Robert Burns, 'O'er the Water to Charlie', in W. Beattie and H. Meikle (eds), *Robert Burns*, London: Penguin, 1946.
7 John Kett, 'The Tawny Owl', in J. Kett, *Tha's a Rum'un, Bor!*, Woodbridge: Baron Publishing [no date – *c*.1973].
8 George Le Bruun, 'It's a great big shame' [song, *c*.1890], taken from W. Matthews, *Cockney Past and Present*, London: Routledge & Kegan Paul, 1938.

9 Devina Symes, 'The Christmas Partee', in *Here in Dorset: Poetry by Devina Symes* [no publisher or date – *c*.1980]; taken from M. Wakelin, *The Southwest of England*, Amsterdam: Benjamins, 1986.

Chapter 3 The Pronunciation of Modern Dialects

1 'I've Just Seen a Face' and 'I Saw Her Standing There', both from *The Beatles Lyrics Complete*, London: Futura, 1974.
2 John Kett, 'An Ordinerry Rood', in J. Kett, *Tha's a Rum'un Tew!*, Woodbridge: Baron Publishing, 1975.

Chapter 4 The Grammar of English Dialects

1 Bill Green, 'A Morning Stroll in May', in *The Dorset Year Book 1982*, Dorset: Society of Dorset Men; taken from M. Wakelin, *The Southwest of England*, Amsterdam: Benjamins, 1986.
2 Charles Benham, 'There's olluz summat', in C. Benham, *Essex Ballads*, Colchester: Benham Newspapers, 1960.
3 Samuel Laycock (1826–93), 'Welcome, Bonny Brid', from *Lyrics of the Cotton Famine;* taken from P. Wright, *Lancashire Dialect*, Clapham, N. Yorks: Dalesman Publishing [no date].
4 'Our Mary's Bonnet', in R. Scollins and J. Titford, *Ey Up, Mi Duck* [notes to record produced by Ram Productions, Ilkeston, Derbyshire, no date].
5 Devina Symes, 'The Christmas Partee', in *Here in Dorset: Poetry by Devina Symes* [no publisher or date – *c*.1980]; taken from M. Wakelin, *The Southwest of England*, Amsterdam, Benjamins, 1986.
6 Ibid.
7 Charles Benham, 'Jim's New Gal', in C. Benham, *Essex Ballads*, Colchester, Benham Newspapers, 1960.
8 Benham, 'Owd Bill', ibid.
9 Benham, 'Tell you for why', ibid.
10 Bernard Moore [S. S. Hunt], 'Riches', from *A Cornish Collection*, London: C. W. Daniel, 1933; taken from M. Wakelin, *The Southwest of England*, Amsterdam: Benjamins, 1986.
11 Edward Garfitt, in *Living Earth*, April–June 1989, p. 11 [found originally a few years ago in *Cotswold Life*].
12 G. E. Campion, 'Noä Callers', in G. E. Campion *Lincolnshire Dialects*, Boston, Lincs: Richard Kay, 20 Sleaford Rd [no date].
13 Edith Waugh [1812–90], 'Come Whoam to thi Childer and Me', taken from P. Wright, *Lancashire Dialect*, Clapham, N. Yorks: Dalesman Publishing [no date].

Sources and Further Reading

◆

Maps 1–8 and 20–3 are based in part on data available in the publications of the *Survey of English Dialects* (*SED*). Maps 25–6, 28–30 and 32 are also derived from materials published by the *SED*. These materials are available in:

H. Orton et al., *Survey of English Dialects: The Basic Material*, 4 vols. Leeds: E. J. Arnold, 1962–71.
H. Orton et al., *The Linguistic Atlas of England*, Edinburgh: Croom Helm, 1978.
H. Orton and N. Wright, A *Word Geography of England*, London: Seminar Press, 1975.

Maps 27 and 33 are based on maps in C. Upton et al., *Word Maps*, Edinburgh: Croom Helm, 1987, which is also derived from *SED* materials.
Maps 10–17 are based on my own researches and on J. C. Wells, *Accents of English*, Cambridge: Cambridge University Press, 1982.
Maps 34–5 are from David North's 'Spatial aspects of linguistic change in Surrey, Kent & Sussex', in W. Viereck (ed.), *Focus on England and Wales*, Amsterdam: Benjamins, 1985.
Map 31 is based on information given in Iona and Peter Opie, *The Lore and Language of Schoolchildren*, Oxford: Oxford University Press, 1959.
Map 24 is based on research carried out for an undergraduate project at the University of Reading by Heather Harris.
The research in Cumbria mentioned on p. 122 was carried out by Alison White, and the double modal examples on pp. 103–4 are from Christine McDonald's 1981 Newcastle University PhD thesis 'Variation in the Use of Modal Verbs with Special Reference to Tyneside'.
Of the many scores of other works that have been consulted in writing this book, the reader might especially like to see:

M. Wakelin, *Focus on the Southwest*, Amsterdam: Benjamins, 1987.

M. Wakelin, *English Dialects: An Introduction*, London: Athlone, 1972.

B. Jones, *The Poems of W. Barnes*, London: Centaur Press, 1962.

Also of interest are:

P. Trudgill and A. Hughes, *English Accents and Dialects*, London: Edward Arnold, 1995.

P. Trudgill (ed.), *Language in the British Isles*, Cambridge: Cambridge University Press, 1985.

Index

$\blacklozenge$